W9-CCQ-117

武士道

Graphic Design by Nancy J. Hom
Photography by Ed Ikuta and Leslie Kim
Cover model—Makoto Ibushi

BUSHIDO
The Warrior's Code

BY INAZO NITOBE

To my beloved uncle
Tokitoshi Ota
who taught me to revere the past
and to admire the deeds of the Samurai
I dedicate this little book

Compiled and Edited by Charles Lucas

© 1979 Ohara Publications, Incorporated
All rights reserved
Printed in the United States of America
Library of Congress Catalog Card Number: 75-21718

ISBN 0-89750-031-8

Thirtieth printing 2000

OHARA 🅿 PUBLICATIONS, INCORPORATED
SANTA CLARITA, CALIFORNIA

Publisher's Preface

For decades, news dispatches from Tokyo, Taiwan, Peking, Seoul, Bangkok and other exotic cities in the Orient were tucked under the general heading of "Notes From The Mysterious East." It was always assumed that the Westerner hadn't a clue as to the reality of what was going on in the Asian mind. Often he hadn't.

The rendering of *kanji* (characters), their written language, is an art form. Their numerical systems boggle the mind. Their attitudes confound us. Surely there must be some means of getting to the basics of, for example, the Japanese mind. One immediately hears mumblings of the word *Bushido*. But what is it? How does one learn anything about it? One hears of some elements of the Code of Bushido getting out of hand, of others disappearing. When either happens, the Japanese seem to be headed for a spate of trouble, and sometimes the rest of the world gets some lumps, too. World War II is an example. Militarism, stemming from exaggerated senses of loyalty and courage and the depletion of other elements of Bushido, accounted for the disastrous wars of conquest in the 1930's and '40's.

In an effort to foster understanding of the basic scope of the Code of Bushido, this book is published. The reader will appreciate learning not just part of the code, but all of it. He will then see that no one element could be dropped or increased. The code was, and still is, a unique set of balances. A thorough reading of this book will give the reader an understanding of this once incomprehensible code, and many of the veils of mystery of the Orient will be lifted.

In 1899, Inazo Nitobe wrote *Bushido, The Soul of Japan*, submitting it for publication at the end of that year. A model of Victorian rhetoric, *Bushido* is also the successful completion of a monumental research task undertaken by the author. Mr. Nitobe searched European archives for original. sources and translated much of the material he chose to use from original Japanese texts.

This republication of the work includes his original text because the publishers feel, and the reader will probably concur, it captures the essence of Bushido at the turn of the century. As one reads through his scholarly and often exhaustive sentences, he experiences something of the stoicism and tenacity required of Bushido. But lasting it out is rewarding. By the time he reaches the end of his text, he will find that the whole subject of Bushido has had a cumulative effect—the reader actually develops a feeling for the concept. Further, he truly understands it.

At the beginning of each of Mr. Nitobe's chapters, we have provided a narrative outline of the points he raises in his text. The reader may find referring back to this introductory preface to the chapter helpful to his comprehension of Mr. Nitobe's material. But the careful reader will wish to absorb the actual text, especially those passages dealing with such romantic subjects as the education of the samurai, the fashioning of the sword and the detailed horror of *hara-kiri* (ritualistic suicide).

Undoubtedly, students of Bushido will wish to debate the subject of the future of the code. Further studies in contemporary Japanese culture are suggested. Movements underway in Japan indicate that, in many areas, there is a marked return to the values of Bushido as they were handed down through the centuries. Many Japanese consider a return to the Code of Bushido to be the salvation of Japan in the last quarter of this century.

Ohara Publications
Burbank, California, 1975

Note. The original Ohara publication of *Bushido* was in 1969.

Author's Preface

In 1889, the distinguished Belgian jurist, M. de Laveleye, turned the conversation to the subject of religion. "Do you mean to say that you have no religious instruction in your schools?" the professor asked. When I explained that there was none, he was astonished. "No religion! How do you impart moral education?" At the time I was at a loss for an answer. The implications of the question had a stunning effect on me. I had no ready answer because the moral precepts I had learned in my childhood days, were not given in schools; they were imparted as part of the feudal tradition that still held sway over much of Japan in my youth. To understand Bushido and the feudal system is essential to a comprehension of the soul of Japan. Without a working knowledge of them, the moral fiber and ideas of present Japan are a sealed book.

All through the work, I have tried to illustrate the points I have made with similar examples from European history and literature. I hope this will make the subject more relative for the comprehension of the Western reader.

In concluding this preface, I wish to express my thanks to my friend Anna C. Hartshorne for many valuable suggestions and for the characteristically Japanese design made by her for the original cover of this book.

About ten years ago, while spending a few days under the hospitable roof of the distinguished Belgian jurist, the lamented M. de Laveleye, our conversation turned during one of our rambles, to the subject of religion. "Do you mean to say," asked the venerable professor, "that you have no religious instruction in your schools?" On my replying in the negative he suddenly halted in astonishment, and in a voice which I shall not easily forget, he repeated "No religion! How do you impart moral education?" The question stunned me at the time. I could give no ready answer, for the moral precepts I learned in my childhood days, were not given in schools; and not until I began to analyze the different elements that formed my moral notions, did I find that it was Bushido that breathed them into my nostrils.

The direct inception of this little book is due to the frequent queries put by my wife as to the reasons why such ideas and customs prevail in Japan.

In my attempts to give satisfactory replies to M. de Laveleye and to my wife, I found that without understanding Feudalism and Bushido,* the moral ideas of the present Japan are a sealed volume.

Taking advantage of enforced idleness on account of long illness, I put down in the order now presented to the public some of the answers given in our household conversation. They consist mainly of what I was taught and told in my youthful days, when Feudalism was still in force.

Between Lafcadio Hearn and Mrs. Hugh Fraser on one side and Sir Ernest Satow and Prof. Chamberlain on the other, it is indeed discouraging to write anything Japanese in English. The only advantage I have over them is that I can assume the attitude of a personal defendant, while these distinguished writers are at best solicitors and attorneys. I have often thought,—"Had I their gift of language, I would present the cause of Japan in more eloquent terms!" But one who speaks in a borrowed tongue should be thankful if he can just make himself intelligible.

All through the discourse I have tried to illustrate whatever points I have made with parallel examples from European history and literature, believing that they will aid in bringing the subject nearer to the comprehension of foreign readers.

Should any of my allusions to religious subjects and to religious

---

* Pronounced Booshee-doh. In putting Japanese words and names into English, Hepburn's rule is followed, that the vowels should be used as in European languages, and the consonants as in English.

workers be thought slighting I trust my attitude towards Christianity itself will not be questioned. It is with ecclesiastical methods and with the forms which obscure the teachings of Christ, and not with the teachings themselves, that I have little sympathy. I believe in the religion taught by Him and handed down to us in the New Testament, as well as in the law written in the heart. Further, I believe that God hath made a testament which may be called "old" with every people and nation,—Gentile or Jew, Christian or Heathen. As to the rest of my theology, I need not impose upon the patience of the public.

In concluding this preface, I wish to express my thanks to my friend Anna C. Hartshorne for many valuable suggestions and for the characteristically Japanese design made by her for the cover of this book.

INAZO NITOBE.

Malvern, Pennsylvania, December 1899.

Contents

. . . a code unuttered and unwritten, possessing all the more powerful sanction of an actual deed . . .

Bushido as an Ethical System

Bu-shi-do *parallels* military-knight-way *in English, although no translation is exact. Basically it embodies a code of daily living for the fighting nobles. At the same time as Bushido was developing, a code of chivalry was being formed in Europe. Under the feudal lords of Europe, adherents to the code of chivalry called their guidelines* Precepts of Knighthood. *Gradually they were set down and passed on. At best, they were little more than outlines of behavior.*

Bushido encompassed a system of moral principles. Those instructed in the code were expected to discipline themselves according to it. The maxims were handed down by word of mouth and by example. One studied with the master and copied him. Sometimes, some of the basic ideas of the Code of Bushido were written, but these usually appeared in letters, poems or songs.

As Bushido developed, a set of Military Statutes (Buké Hatto) *was published in a pamphlet form. But it could hardly be called a* true military code, much less a formalization of the Code of Bushido. The contents of the pamphlet dealt with such subjects as marriage, castles, alliances, leagues, recruiting, travel and the like. In all, only 13 subjects were covered. No code of honor was included.

Bushido's growth and the rise of military feudalism in Japan went hand in hand. The formulation of Bushido took centuries. So it is impossible to say when it actually was fully under way. Several generations of military careers had come and gone before Bushido was a concept of sufficient scope to be formally studied. It is similar, in some ways, to early English Common Law—understood but not written down in specific codes. It differs sharply from the concept of English Law, however, because nothing in it compares to the doctrines of the Magna Carta and the Habeus Corpus Act that guaranteed individual rights and have since served as principal sources for civil liberties.

There is no single source for Bushido. Rather, it stems from the same intricate strands that created the fabric of feudalism. English feudalism grew out of the Norman Conquest. Japanese feudalism followed the ascendency of Yoritomo, one of the most remarkable feudal warlords of Japan.

With the rise of feudalism a professional warrior class emerged, similar in many ways to the English knights. These Japanese warriors functioned as guards and attendants and carried the title bu-ki or bu-shi (fighting knights). Fighting was their only vocation. Obviously, they were a rugged breed of men. They had great responsibilities, great honor and privileges and were loyal to their clan or region, as well as their leader. They were also a belligerent lot, needing instruction in courtly manners.

In Christian countries, convenient concessions to chivalry were made. Religion, war and glory served as three essential parts to the soul of the Christian knight. The Japanese samurai learned the code of Bushido, a code far more complicated than that of the Christian knights.

BUSHIDO AS AN ETHICAL SYSTEM

Chivalry is a flower no less native to the soil of Japan than its emblem, the cherry blossom; nor is it a dried-up specimen of an antique virtue preserved in the herbarium of our history. It is still a living object of power and beauty among us; and if it assumes no tangible shape or form, it still scents the moral atmosphere, and makes us aware that we are still under its potent spell. The conditions of society which brought it forth and nourished it have long disappeared; but as those far-off stars, which once were and are not, still continue to shed their rays upon us, so the light of chivalry, which was a child of feudalism, still illuminates our moral path, surviving its mother institution.

It argues a sad defect of information concerning the Far East, when so erudite a scholar as Dr. George Miller did not hesitate to affirm that chivalry, or any other similar institution, has never existed either among the nations of antiquity or among the modern Orientals.* Such ignorance, however, is amply excusable, as the third edition of the good Doctor's work appeared the same year that Commodore Perry was knocking at the gates of our exclusivism. More than a decade later, about the time that our feudalism was in the last throes of existence, Karl Marx, writing *Das Kapital*, called the attention of his readers to the peculiar advantage of studying the social and political institutions of feudalism, as then to be seen in living form only in Japan. I would likewise point the Western historical and ethical student to the study of chivalry in the Japan of the present.

Enticing as is a historical debate on the comparison between European and Japanese feudalism and chivalry, it is not the purpose of this book to enter into it at length. My attempt is rather to relate, *firstly*, the origin and sources of our chivalry; *secondly*, its character and teaching; *thirdly*, its influence among the masses; and, *fourthly*, the continuity and permanence of its influence. Of these several points, the first will be only brief and cursory, or else I should have to take my readers into the devious paths of our national history; the second will be dwelt upon at greater length, as being most likely to interest students in our ways of thought and action; and the rest will be dealt with as corollaries.

The Japanese word, which I have roughly rendered Chivalry, is, in the original, more expressive than Horsemanship. *Bu-shi-do* means literally Military-Knight-Ways—the ways which fighting nobles should observe in their daily life as well as in their vocation; in a word, the "Precepts of Knighthood," the *noblesse oblige* of the warrior class. Having thus given its literal significance, I may be

---

* History Philosophically Illustrated, (3rd Ed., 1853), Vol. II, p. 2.

allowed henceforth to use the word in the original. The use of the original term is also advisable for this reason, that a teaching so circumscribed and unique, engendering a cast of mind and character so peculiar, so local, must wear the badge of its singularity on its face. Some words have a national *timbre* so expressive of race characteristics that the best of translators can do them but scant justice.

Bushido is the code of moral principles which the knights were required or instructed to observe. It is not a written code; at best it consists of a few maxims handed down from mouth to mouth or coming from the pen of some well-known warrior. More frequently it is a code unuttered and unwritten, possessing all the more the powerful sanction of an actual deed, and of a law written on the tablets of the heart. It was founded not on the creation of one brain, however able, or on the life of a single person. It was an organic growth of decades and centuries of military careers. It, perhaps, fills the same position in the history of ethics that the English Constitution does in political history; yet it has had nothing to compare with the Magna Carta or the Habeas Corpus Act. True, early in the seventeenth century Military Statues *(Buké Hatto)* were promulgated; but their thirteen short articles were taken up mostly with marriages, castles, leagues, etc., and didactic regulations were but meagerly touched upon. We cannot, therefore, point out any definite time and place and say, "Here is its fountainhead." Only as it attains consciousness in the feudal age, its origin, in respect to time, may be identified with feudalism. But feudalism itself is woven of many threads, and Bushido shares its intricate nature. As in England the political institutions of feudalism may be said to date from the Norman Conquest, so we may say that in Japan its rise was simultaneous with the ascendancy of Yoritomo, late in the twelfth century. As, however, in England, we find the social elements of feudalism far back in the period previous to William the Conqueror, so, too, the germs of feudalism in Japan had been long existent before the period I have mentioned.

Again, in Japan as in Europe, when feudalism was formally inaugurated, the professional class of warriors naturally came into prominence. These were known as *samurai*, meaning literally, like the old English *cniht* (knecht, knight), guards or attendants—resembling in character the *soldurii*, whom Caesar mentioned as existing in Aquitania, or the *miliets medii* that one reads about in the history of Mediaeval Europe. A Sini-Japanese word *Bu-kè* or *Bu-shi* (Fighting Knights) was also adopted in common use. They were a privileged class, and must originally have been a rough breed who made fighting their vocation. Coming to profess great honor and great privileges, and correspondingly great responsibilities, they soon felt the need of a common standard of behavior, especially as they were always on a belligerent footing and belonged to different clans.

Fair play in fight! What fertile germs of morality lie in this primitive sense of savagery and childhood. Is it not the root of all military and civic virtues? We smile (as if we had outgrown it!) at the boyish desire of the small Britisher, Tom Brown, "to leave behind him the name of a fellow who never bullied a little boy or turned his back on a big one." And yet, who does not know that this desire is the corner-stone on which moral structures of mighty dimensions can be reared? May I not go even so far as to say that the gentlest and most peace-loving of religions endorses this aspiration? The desire of Tom's is the basis on which the greatness of England is largely built, and it will not take us long to discover that *Bushido* does not stand on a lesser pedestal. If fighting in itself, be it offensive or defensive, is, as Quakers rightly testify, brutal and wrong, we can still say with Lessing, "We know from what failings our virtue springs." Childhood begins life with these notions, and knighthood also; but, as life grows larger and its relations many-sided, the early faith seeks sanction from higher authority and more rational sources for its own justification, satisfaction and development. If military systems had operated alone, without higher moral support, how far short of chivalry would the ideal of knighthood have fallen! In Europe, Christianity, interpreted with concessions convenient to chivalry, infused it nevertheless with spiritual data. "Religion, war and glory were the three souls of a perfect Christian knight," says Lamartine. In Japan, Bushido came into being from a more complex set of sources.

. . the human heart, . . . when perfectly placid and clear, reflects the very image of the Diety.

Sources of Bushido

Buddhism had these basic tenets: Sense of calm, trust in fate, submission to the inevitable, disdain of life coupled to friendliness with death, and a stoic composure in the face of calamity. These are all embodied in the code of Bushido.

Beyond the ultimate of the art of swordsmanship stands Zen. Simply put, Zen means applying human effort to reach through meditation zones of thought beyond the range of verbal expression. The method of Zen is contemplation and the achievement of excellence. One of the highest attainments of a master in any of the military arts was to also become a Zen master.

Shintoism means loyalty to the sovereign, reverence for ancestral memory, filial piety. Shintoism imparted passivity to the otherwise arrogant character of the samurai.

In Shintoism there is no original sin, only God-like purity of the human soul. The Shinto temple is devoid of trappings of worship. In the sanctuary there is placed only a plain mirror to typify the human heart when perfectly placid and clear. The mirror reflects the image of the deity. In a sense similar to the Greek philosophy the viewer is admonished, "Know thyself," meaning his moral nature.

The morality of Shintoism is observable in the national consciousness of Japan. Ancestor worship made the Imperial family the fountainhead of the whole nation.

Nature worship endeared the country to the innermost reaches of men's souls. The country became more than the source of gold, grain and life. It became the sacred abode of the gods. Over it ruled the Emperor, a bodily representative of heaven on earth.

Shintoism is comprised of patriotism and loyalty. More than a doctrine, it is the expression of a national impulse.

Confucius was one of the most prolific sources of Bushido. His enunciation of the five moral relationships are foundations in the code of Bushido. The five are: master and servant (governor and governed), father—son, husband—wife, older—younger brothers and friend with friend.

The practice of Shintoism was well suited to the formal ruling *class of samurai warrior-statesmen. Some of Mencius' democratic theories were utilized, but he was generally regarded as a subversive influence.*

An intellectual knowledge of Confucius or Mencius was regarded as ridiculous. Knowledge had to be assimilated and show itself in the character of the learner. Intellect was subordinate to ethical emotion. The Bushido code required knowledge to be a means to the attainment of wisdom. It was never an end in itself.

Knowledge was identical with its practical application in life. Wan Yang Ming was fond of saying, "To know and to act are one and the same." This influential philosopher also said, "The lord of heaven and earth, of all living beings, dwelling in the heart of man, becomes his mind (kokoro); hence a mind is a living thing and is never luminous."

Shinto, and similarly Bushido, subscribed to the doctrine of infallibility of conscience. One must be able to perceive right from wrong and psychical phenomena from physical facts.

SOURCES OF BUSHIDO

Buddhism furnished a sense of calm trust in Fate, a quiet submission to the inevitable, a stoic composure in sight of danger or calamity, a disdain of life and friendliness with death. A foremost teacher of swordsmanship, when he saw his pupil master the utmost of his art, told him, "Beyond this my instruction must give way to Zen teaching." "Zen" is the Japanese equivalent for the Dhyana, which "represents human effort to reach through meditation zones of thought beyond the range of verbal expression."* Its method is contemplation, and its intent, as far as I understand it, to be convinced of a principle that underlies all phenomena, and, if it can, of the Absolute itself, and thus to put oneself in harmony with this Absolute. Thus defined, the teaching was more than the dogma of a sect, and whoever attains to the perception of the Absolute raises himself above worldly things and awakes, like Teufelsdröckh, "to a new Heaven and a new Earth."

What Buddhism failed to give, Shintoism offered in abundance. Such loyalty to the sovereign, such reverence for ancestral memory, and such filial piety as are not taught by any other creed,

*Lafcadio Hearn, Exotics and Retrospectives, p. 84.

were inculcated by the Shinto doctrines, imparting passivity to the otherwise arrogant character of the samurai. Shinto theology has no place for the dogma of "original sin." On the contrary, it believes in the innate goodness and God-like purity of the human soul, adoring it as the innermost sanctuary from which divine oracles are proclaimed. Everybody has observed that the Shinto shrines are conspicuously devoid of objects and instruments of worship, and that a plain mirror hung in the sanctuary forms the essential part of its furnishing. The presence of this article is easy to explain: it typifies the human heart, which, when perfectly placid and clear, reflects the very image of the Deity. When you stand, therefore, in front of the shrine to worship, you see your own image reflected on its shining surface, and the act of worship is tantamount to the old Delphic injunction, "Know Thyself." But self-knowledge does not imply, either in the Greek or Japanese teaching, knowledge of the physical part of man, not his anatomy or his psycho-physics; knowledge was to be of a moral kind, the introspection of our moral nature. Mommsen, comparing the Greek and the Roman, says that when the former worshipped he raised his eyes to heaven, for his prayer was contemplation, while the latter veiled his head, for his was reflection. Essentially like the Roman conception of religion, our reflection brought into prominence not so much the moral as the national consciousness of the individual. Its nature-worship endeared the country to our inmost souls, while its ancestor-worship, tracing from lineage to lineage, made the Imperial family the fountainhead of the whole nation. To us the country is more than land and soil from which to mine gold or to reap grain — it is the sacred abode of the gods, the spirits of our forefathers: to us the Emperor is more than the Arch Constable of a *Rechtsstaat*, or even the Patron of a *Kulturstaat* — he is the bodily representative of Heaven on earth, blending in his person its power and its mercy.

The tenets of Shintoism cover the two predominating features of the emotional life of our race — patriotism and loyalty. Arthur May Knapp very truly says: "In Hebrew literature it is often difficult to tell whether the writer is speaking of God or of the Commonwealth; of Heaven or of Jerusalem; of the Messiah or of the nation itself."* A similar confusion may be noticed in the nomenclature of our national faith. I said confusion, because it

*"Feudal and Modern Japan," Vol. I, p. 183.

will be so deemed by a logical intellect on account of its verbal ambiguity; still, being a framework of national instinct and race feelings, it never pretends to systematic philosophy or a rational theology. This religion — or, is it not more correct to say, the race emotions which this religion expressed? — thoroughly imbued Bushido with loyalty to the sovereign and love of country. These acted more as impulses than as doctrines.

As to strictly ethical doctrines, the teachers of Confucius were the most prolific source of Bushido. His enunciation of the five moral relations between *master and servant* (the governing and the governed), *father and son, husband and wife, older and younger brother*, and between *friend and friend*, was but a confirmation of what the race instinct had recognized before his writings were introduced from China. The calm, benignant, and comfortable character of his politico-ethical precepts was particularly well suited to the samurai, who formed the ruling class. His aristocratic and conservative tone was well adapted to the requirements of these warrior statesmen. Next to Confucius, Mencius exercised an immense authority over Bushido. His forcible and often quite democratic theories were exceedingly taking to sympathetic natures, and they were even thought dangerous to, and subversive of, the existing social order, hence his works were for a long time under censure. Still, the words of this mastermind found permanent lodgment in the heart of the samurai.

The writing of Confucius and Mencius formed the principal text-books for youths and the highest authority in discussion among the old. A mere acquaintance with the classics of these two sages was held, however, in no high esteem. A common proverb ridicules one who has only an intellectual knowledge of Confucius, as a man ever studious but ignorant of *Analects*. A typical samurai calls a literary savant a book-smelling sot. Another compares learning to an ill-smelling vegetable that must be boiled and boiled before it is fit for use. A man who has read little smells a little pedantic, and a man who has read much smells yet more so; both are alike unpleasant. The writer meant thereby that *knowledge becomes really such only when it is assimilated in the mind of the learner and shows in his character.* An intellectual specialist was considered a machine. Intellect itself was considered subordinate to ethical emotion. Man and the universe were conceived to be alike spiritually and ethically. Bushido could not accept the judgment of Huxley, that the cosmic process was immoral.

Bushido made light of knowledge as such. It was not pursued as an end in itself, but as a means to the attainment of wisdom. Hence, he who stopped short of this end was regarded no higher than a convenient machine, which could turn out poems and maxims at bidding. Thus, knowledge was conceived as identical with its practical application in life; and this Socratic doctrine found its greatest exponent in the Chinese philosopher, Wan Yang Ming, who never wearies of repeating, "To know and to act are one and the same."

I beg leave for a moment's digression while I am on this subject, inasmuch as some of the noblest types of *bushi* were strongly influenced by the teachings of this sage. Western readers will easily recognize in his writing many parallels to the New Testament. Making allowance for the terms peculiar to either teaching, the passage, "Seek ye first the kingdom of God and his righteousness; and all these things shall be added unto you," conveys a thought that may be found on almost any page of Wan Yang Ming. A Japanese disciple* of his says — "The lord of Heaven and Earth, of all living beings, dwelling in the heart of man, becomes his mind *(Kokoro):* hence a mind is a living thing, and is ever luminous:" and again, "The spiritual light of our essential being is pure, and is not affected by the will of man. Spontaneously springing up in our mind, it shows what is right and wrong: it is then called conscience; it is even the light that proceedeth from the god of heaven." I am inclined to think that the Japanese mind, as expressed in the simple tenets of the Shinto religion, was particularly open to the reception of Yang Ming's precepts. He carried his doctrine of the infallibility of conscience to extreme transcendentalism, attributing to it the faculty to perceive, not only the distinction between right and wrong, but also the nature of psychical facts and physical phenomena. He went as far as, if not farther than, Berkeley and Fichte, in Idealism, denying the existence of things outside of human ken. If his system had all the logical errors charged to Solipsism, it had all the efficacy of strong conviction, and its moral import in developing individuality of character and equanimity of temper cannot be denied.

Thus, whatever the sources, the essential principles which *Bushido* imbibed from them and assimilated to itself, were few and simple.

*Miwa Shissai.

. . . *to die when it is right to die, to strike when to strike is right.*

Rectitude or Justice

Rectitude means correct judgment or procedure for the resolution of righteousness. "To die when it is right to die, to strike when it is right to strike," are axioms in this portion of the code.

Rectitude has been compared to the firmness of a skeleton. As the skeleton gives shape, firmness and stature to the body, rectitude forms the core of the samurai. Without such a core no amount of training can convert a human frame into an honorable warrior.

Gishi (a man of rectitude) was an honorable title bestowed on those who had mastered the art of rectitude.

Valor is rectitude's twin. Together these two elements provide the courage to right a wrong. The need to do so stems from a sense of gi-ri (right reason). This became giri and originally meant duty. But it was an unshirkable duty. In later eras giri was over-emphasized at the expense of right reason (sensibility). Such usage *compelled a daughter to sell her chastity to pay for her father's dissipation. This was a perversion of the term. Later it was taken to mean only a sense of obligation or the obligation itself. Finally, giri was the duty of an individual to courageously use correct judgment for an ennobling cause.*

RECTITUDE OR JUSTICE

Justice is the most cogent precept in the code of the samurai. Nothing is more loathsome to him than under-hand dealings and crooked undertakings. The conception of rectitude may be erroneous — it may be narrow. A well-known bushi defines it as a power of resolution; — "Rectitude is the power of deciding upon a certain course of conduct in accordance with reason, without wavering; — to die when it is right to die, to strike when to strike is right." Another speaks of it in the following terms: "Rectitude is the bone that gives firmness and stature. As without bones the head cannot rest on the top of the spine, nor hands move nor feet stand, so without rectitude neither talent nor learning can make of a human frame a samurai. With it the lack of accomplishments is as nothing." Even in the latter days of feudalism, when the long continuance of peace brought leisure into the life of the warrior class, and with it dissipations of all kinds and accomplishments of gentle arts, the epithet *Gishi* (a man of rectitude) was considered superior to any name that signified mastery of learning or art. The Forty-seven Faithfuls — of whom so much is made in our popular education — are known in common parlance as the Forty-seven *Gishi*.

In times when cunning artifice was liable to pass for military tact and downright falsehood for *ruse de guerre*, this manly virtue, frank and honest, was a jewel that shone the brightest and was most highly praised. Rectitude is a twin brother to valor, another martial virtue. But before proceeding to speak of valor, let me linger a little while on what I may term a derivation from rectitude, which, deviating slightly from its original, became more and more removed from it, until its meaning was perverted in the popular acceptance. I speak of *gi-ri*, literally the right reason, but which came in time to mean a vague sense of duty which public opinion expects an incumbent to fulfill. In its original and unalloyed sense, it meant duty, pure and simple, — hence, we speak of the *giri* we owe to parents, to superiors, to inferiors, to society at large, and so forth. In these instances *giri* is duty; for what else is duty than what right reason demands and commands us to do. Should not right reason be our categorical imperative?

Giri primarily meant no more than duty, and I dare say its etymology was derived from the fact that in our conduct, say to our parents, though love should be the only motive, lacking that, there must be some other authority to enforce filial piety; and they formulated this authority in *giri*. Very rightly did they formulate this authority — *giri* — since if love does not rush to deeds of virtue, recourse must be had to man's intellect and his reason must be quickened to convince him of the necessity of acting correctly. The same is true of any other moral obligation. The instant duty become onerous, right reason steps in to prevent our shirking it. *Giri* thus understood is a severe taskmaster, with a birch-rod in his hand to make sluggards perform their part. It is a secondary power in ethics; as a motive it is infinitely inferior to the Christian doctrine of love, which should be *the* law. I deem it a product of the conditions of an artificial society — of a society in which accident of birth and unmerited favour instituted class distinctions, in which the family was the social unit, in which seniority of age was of more account than superiority of talents, in which natural affections had often to succumb before arbitrary man-made customs. Because of this very artificiality, *giri* in time degenerated into a vague sense of propriety called up to explain this and sanction that, — as, for example, why a mother must, if need be, sacrifice all her other children in order to save the first-born; or why a daughter must sell her chastity to get funds to pay for the father's dissipation, and the like. Starting as right reason, *giri* has, in my opinion, often stooped to casuistry. It has even degenerated into cowardly fear of censure. I might say of *giri* what Scott wrote of patriotism, that "as it is the fairest, so it is often the most suspicious, mask of other feelings." Carried beyond or below right reason, *giri* became a monstrous misnomer. It harbored under its wings every sort of sophistry and hypocrisy. It would have been easily turned into a nest of cowardice, if Bushido had not a keen and correct sense of courage.

"... *it is true courage to live when it is right to live, and to die only when it is right to die.*"

Courage, the Spirit of Daring

Courage is a virtue only in the cause of righteousness. Death for an unworthy cause was termed a dog's death. A prince of Mito once said, "It is true courage to live when it is right to live, and to die only when it is right to die."

Valor, fortitude, bravery, fearlessness and courage were the qualities of soul most appealing to the minds of young boys. Stories of military exploits abounded. The stereotype of Spartan courage and of ignoring pain was indoctrinated into the children from the time of their birth. The fledgling samurai with an empty stomach knew it was a disgrace to feel the pangs of hunger. During training they were subjected to periods of deprivation of food and exposure to extreme cold. Endurance was the hallmark of a successful novice.

The young students often read for long periods in the early morning. This was a must before breakfast. They walked barefoot to their teachers. Once or twice a month there was a festival to a god of learning. The youths spent the night without sleeping. In small groups they managed to stay awake by reading aloud to each other.

Pilgrimages were made to uncanny places such as graveyards, haunted houses and public execution grounds. During the days of public executions the youngster witnessed the decapitations. Then, during the night they had to come back to the site and leave their marks on the trunkless head.

Thus was courage and the spirit of daring made a part of the training and soul of the fledgling samurai.

COURAGE, THE SPIRIT OF DARING AND BEARING

Courage was scarcely deemed worthy to be counted among virtues, unless it was exercised in the cause of Righteousness. In his *Analects* Confucius defines Courage by explaining as he often did, what its negative is. "Perceiving what is right," he says, "and doing it not, argues lack of courage." Put this epigram into a positive statement, and it runs, "Courage is doing what is right." To run all kinds of hazards, to jeopardize one's self, to rush into the jaws of death — these are too often identified with Valor, and in the profession of arms such rashness of conduct — what Shakespeare calls "valor misbegot" — is unjustly applauded; but not so in the Precepts of Knighthood. Death for a cause unworthy of dying for, was called a "dog's death." "To rush into the thick of battle and to be slain in it," says a Prince of Mito, "is easy enough, and the merest churl is equal to the task; but," he continues, "it is true courage to live when it is right to live, and to die only when it is right to die." A distinction which is made in the West between moral and physical courage has long been recognized among us. What samurai youth has not heard of "Great Valor" and the "Valor of a Villain?"

Valor, Fortitude, Bravery, Fearlessness, Courage, being the qualities of soul which appeal most easily to juvenile minds, and which can be trained by exercise and example, were, so to speak, the most popular virtues, early emulated among the youth. Stories of military exploits were repeated almost before boys left their mother's breast. Does a little baby cry for any ache? The mother scolds him in this fashion: "What a coward to cry for a trifling pain! What will you do when your arm is cut off in battle? What when you are called upon to commit *harakiri?*" We all know the pathetic fortitude of a famished little boy-prince of Sendai, who in the drama is made to say to his little page, "Seest thou those tiny sparrows in the nest, how their yellow bills are opened wide, and now see! There comes their mother with grains to feed them. How eagerly and happily the little ones eat! But for a samurai, when his stomach is empty, it is a disgrace to feel hunger." Anecdotes of fortitude and bravery abound in nursery tales, though stories of this kind are not by any means the only method of early imbuing the spirit with daring and fearlessness. Parents, with sternness sometimes verging on cruelty, set their children to tasks that called forth all the pluck that was in them. "Bears hurl their cubs down the gorge," they said. Samurai's sons were let down to steep valleys of hardship, and spurred to Herculean tasks. Occasional deprivation of food or exposure to cold, was considered a highly efficacious test for hardening them to endurance. Children of tender age were sent among utter strangers with some message to deliver, were made to rise before the sun, and before breakfast attend to their reading exercises, walking to their teachers with bare feet in the cold of winter; they frequently — once or twice a month, as on the festival of a god of learning, — came together in small groups and passed the night without sleep, in reading aloud by turns. Pilgrimages to all sorts of uncanny places — to execution grounds, to graveyards, to houses reputed to be haunted, were favourite pastimes of youths. In the days when decapitation was public, not only were small boys sent to witness the ghastly scene, but they were made to visit alone the place in the darkness of night and there to leave a mark of their visit on the trunkless head.

Does this ultra-Spartan system of "drilling the nerves" strike the modern teacher with horror and doubt — doubt whether the tendency would not be brutalizing, nipping in the bud the tender emotions of the heart? The system was thought to be only an essential part of the education of a samurai.

"The feeling of distress is the root of benevolence."

Benevolence, the Feeling of Distress

Love, affection for others, sympathy and nobility of feeling were regarded as the highest attributes of the soul. Benevolence kept feudalism from sinking into total militarism. Rectitude and stern justice were masculine traits; mercy and gentleness were thought of as feminine characteristics. But both were regarded as essential to a balanced life. Bushi no Nasaki *(the tenderness of a warrior)* was a trait to cultivate. Mercy could not stem from a blind impulse. It must be rendered with due regard to justice and backed with the power to save or kill.

Samurai agreed with Mencius (Meng-tzu or Meng-tse) who taught, "Benevolence brings under its sway whatever hinders its power, just as water subdues fire. A feeling of distress is the root of benevolence." This bears a striking resemblance to Adam Smith's ethical philosophy founded on sympathy.

Gentleness and high manners were taught to the warrior class. The warriors were encouraged to study music and poetry. In music they were urged to master the biwa *(a guitar-like instrument)* rather than drums or trumpets. The loose translation of a typical verse attributed to a Prince of Shirakawa reads, "Though they may wound your feelings, these three you have only to forgive, the breeze that scatters your flowers, the cloud that hides your moon and the man who tries to pick a quarrel with you."

In Europe, Christianity roused compassion amidst the horrors of war. In Japan, love, music and letters accomplished a similar result.

BENEVOLENCE, THE FEELING
OF DISTRESS

The capacity to express love, affection for others, sympathy and pity were recognized as supreme virtues of the human soul. The quality had to be tempered with objectivity. It was deemed a princely virtue in a twofold sense; — princely among the manifold attributes of a noble spirit; princely as particularly befitting a princely profession. We needed no Shakespeare to feel — though, perhaps, like the rest of the world, we needed him to express it — that mercy became a monarch better than his crown. Under the regime of feudalism which could easily degenerate into militarism it was to Benevolence that we owed our deliverance from despotism of the worst kind. We knew it was a tender virtue and motherlike. If upright Rectitude and stern Justice were peculiarly masculine, Mercy had the gentleness and the persuasion of a feminine nature. We were warned against indulging in indiscriminate charity, without seasoning it with justice and rectitude. Masamuné expressed it well in his oft-quoted aphorism — "Rectitude carried to excess hardens into stiffness; Benevolence indulged beyond measure sinks into weakness."

Fortunately Mercy was not so rare as it was beautiful, for it is universally true that "The bravest are the tenderest, the loving are the daring." *"Bushi no nasaké"* — the tenderness of a warrior — had a sound which appealed at once to whatever was noble in us; not that the mercy of a samurai was generically different from the mercy of any other being, but because it implied mercy where mercy was not a blind impulse, but where it recognized due regard to justice, and where mercy did not remain merely a certain state of mind, but where it was backed with power to save or kill. As economists speak of demand as being effectual or ineffectual, similarly we may call the mercy of bushi effectual, since it implied the power of acting for the good or detriment of the recipient.

Priding themselves as they did in their brute strength and privileges to turn it into account, the samurai gave full consent to what Mencius taught concerning the power of Love. "Benevolence," he says, "brings under its sway whatever hinders its power, just as water subdues fire: they only doubt the power of water to quench flames who try to extinguish with a cupful a whole burning wagon-load of fagots." He also says that "the feeling of distress is the root of benevolence," therefore a benevolent man is ever mindful of those who are suffering and in distress. Thus did Mencius long anticipate Adam Smith who founds his ethical philosophy on Sympathy.

It is indeed striking how closely the code of knightly honour of one country coincides with that of others; in other words, how the much-abused oriental ideas of morale find their counterparts in those of the European.

Benevolence to the weak, the down-trodden or the vanquished, was ever extolled as peculiarly becoming to a samurai. Lovers of Japanese art must be familiar with the representation of a priest riding backwards on a cow. The rider was once a warrior who in his day made his name a by-word of terror. In that terrible battle of Sumano-ura, (1184 A. D.) which was one of the most decisive in our history, he overtook an enemy and in single combat had him in the clutch of his gigantic arms. Now the etiquette of war required that on such occasions no blood should be spilt, unless the weaker party proved to be a man of rank or ability equal to that of the stronger. The grim combatant would have the name of the man under him; but he refusing to make it known, his helmet was ruthlessly torn off, when the sight of a juvenile face, fair and beardless, made the astonished knight relax his hold. Helping the youth to his feet, in paternal tones he bade the stripling go: "Off, young prince, to thy mother's side! The sword of Kumagaye shall never be tarnished by a drop of thy blood. Haste and flee o'er yon pass before thy enemies come in sight!" The young warrior refused to go and begged Kumagaye, for the honor of both, to dispatch him on the spot. Above the hoary head of the veteran gleams the cold blade, which many a time before has sundered the chords of life, but his stout heart quails; there flashes athwart his mental eye the vision of his own boy, who this self-same day marched to the sound of bugle to try his maiden arms; the strong hand of the warrior quivers; again he begs his victim to flee for his life. Finding all his entreaties vain and hearing the approaching steps of his comrades, he exclaims: "If thou art overtaken, thou mayest fall at a more ignoble hand than mine. O, thou Infinite! receive his soul!" In an instant the sword flashes in the air, and when it falls it is red with adolescent blood. When the war is ended, we find our soldier returning in triumph, but little cares he now for honor or fame; he renounces his warlike career, shaves his head, dons a priestly garb, devotes the rest of his days to holy pilgrimage, never turning his back to the West, where lies the Paradise whence salvation comes and whither the sun hastes daily for his rest.

Critics may point out flaws in this story, which is casuistically vulnerable. Let it be: all the same it shows that Tenderness, Pity and Love, were traits which adorned the most sanguinary exploits of a samurai. In the principality of Satsuma, noted for its martial spirit and education, the custom prevailed for young men to practice music; not the blast of trumpets or the beat of drums, — "those clamorous harbingers of blood and death" — stirring us to imitate the actions of a tiger, but sad and tender melodies on the *biwa*,* soothing our fiery spirits, drawing our thoughts away from scent of blood and scenes of carnage. Polybius tells us of the Constitution of Arcadia, which required all youths under thirty to practice music, in order that this gentle art might alleviate the rigors of the inclement region. It is to its influence that he attributes the absence of cruelty in that part of the Arcadian mountains.

Nor was Satsuma the only place in Japan where gentleness was inculcated among the warrior class. A prince of Shirakawa jots down his random thoughts, and among them is the following: "Though they come stealing to your bedside in the silent watches of the night, drive not away, but rather cherish these — the fragrance of flowers, the sound of distant bells, the insect hummings of a frosty night." And again, "Though they may wound your feelings, these three you have only to forgive, the breeze that scatters your flowers, the cloud that hides your moon, and the man who tries to pick quarrels with you."

It was ostensibly to express, but actually to cultivate, these gentler emotions that the writing of verses was encouraged. Our poetry has therefore a strong undercurrent of pathos and tenderness. A well-known anecdote of a rustic samurai illustrates a case in point. When he was told to learn versification, and "The Warbler's Notes"† was given him for the subject of his first

---

*A musical instrument, resembling the guitar.

† The Uguisu or Warbler, sometimes called the nightingale of Japan.

attempt, his fiery spirit rebelled and he flung at the feet of his master this uncouth production, which ran

> "The brave warrior keeps apart
> The ear that might listen
> To the warbler's song."

His master, undaunted by the crude sentiment, continued to encourage the youth, until one day the music of his soul was awakened to respond to the sweet notes of the *uguisu*, and he wrote

> "Stands the warrior, mailed and strong,
> To hear the Uguisu's song,
> Warbled sweet the trees among."

We admire and enjoy the heroic incident in Körner's short life, when, as he lay wounded on the battle-field, he scribbled his famous "Farewell to Life." Incidents of a similar kind were not at all unusual in our warfare. Our pithy, epigrammatic poems were particularly well suited to the improvisation of a single sentiment. Everybody of any education was either a poet or a would be poet. Not infrequently a marching soldier might be seen to halt, taking his writing utensils from his belt, and compose an ode, — and such papers were found afterward in the helmets or the breast-plates when these were removed from their lifeless wearers.

What Christianity has done in Europe toward rousing compassion in the midst of belligerent horrors, love of music and letters has done in Japan. The cultivation of tender feelings breeds considerate regard for the sufferings of others. Modesty and complaisance, actuated by respect for others' feelings, are at the root of politeness.

. . . the outward manisfestation of a sympathetic regard for the feelings of others.

Politeness

The most casual visitor to Japan immediately observes politeness, courtesy and excellent manners. They are part of the Japanese way of life.

According to the code of Bushido, politeness is a poor virtue if it is actuated only by a fear of offending good taste. Rather, it should stem from a sympathetic regard for the feelings of others. In its highest form politeness approaches love. Yet, no virtue stands alone. One guards against an extreme degree of politeness.

A sense of propriety stands at the pinnacle of social intercourse.

An elaborate system of etiquette was developed to train youth. Manners grew to become a science. Bowing, walking, standing, table manners and tea serving were developed as ritual ceremonies.

On the surface such attention to the details of life's niceties seemed tedious to the novice samurai. But soon they discovered that such adherence to the rituals saved time and labor. The trappings of the ceremonies proved to be the most economical and graceful ways of learning the application of force. According to Ogasawara, "The end of all etiquette is to so cultivate your mind that even when you are quietly seated, not the roughest ruffian can dare make onset on your person."

Etiquette perfectly harmonized the total being with himself and his environment, and expressed mastery of the spirit over the flesh.

Gracefulness represented economy of force. Therefore, it provided a reservoir of force. Fine manners meant power in repose.

The tea ceremony directed a person's thoughts away from the world. As such it was a method to achieve discipline of the soul.

Politeness is activated by tender feelings toward the sensibilities of others. Weep with those who weep; rejoice with those who rejoice.

The exchange of gifts in Japan is a perfect example of politeness. When the westerner presents a gift he does so because it has an intrinsic value and certain attributes. It expressed the giver's appreciation of the recipient. In Japan any gift would be unworthy. Therefore it must be regarded as having no intrinsic value or attribute. It serves only as a token.

Should one tell the truth or be polite? In Japan the custom of replying to this question differs sharply from what the westerner would reply.

POLITENESS

Politeness is a poor virtue, if it is actuated only by a fear of offending good taste, whereas it should be the outward manifestation of a sympathetic regard for the feelings of others. It also implies a due regard for the fitness of things, therefore due respect to social positions; for these latter express no plutocratic distinctions, but were originally distinctions for actual merit.

In its highest form, politeness almost approaches love. We may reverently say, politeness "suffers long, and is kind; envies not, vaunts not itself, is not puffed up; does not behave itself unseemly, seeks not her own, is not easily provoked, takes not account of evil." Is it any wonder that Professor Dean, in speaking of the six elements of Humanity, accords to Politeness an exalted position, inasmuch as it is the ripest fruit of social intercourse?

While thus extolling Politeness, far be it from me to put it in the front rank of virtues. If we analyze it, we shall find it correlated with other virtues of a higher order; for what virtue stands alone? While — or rather because — it was exalted as peculiar to the profession of arms, and as such esteemed in a degree higher than its deserts, there came into existence its counterfeits. Confucius himself has repeatedly taught that external appurtenances are as little a part of propriety as sounds are of music.

When propriety was elevated to the *sine qua non* of social intercourse, it was only to be expected that an elaborate system of etiquette should come into vogue to train youth in correct social behavior. How one must bow in meeting others, how he must walk and sit, were taught and learned with utmost care. Table manners grew to be a science. Tea serving and drinking were raised to ceremony. A man of education is, of course, expected to be master of all these.

I have heard slighting remarks made by Europeans upon our elaborate discipline of politeness. It has been criticized as absorbing too much of our thought and in so far a folly to observe strict obedience to it. I admit that there may be unnecessary niceties in ceremonious etiquette, but whether it partakes as much of folly as the adherence to ever-changing fashions of the West, is a question not very clear to my mind. Even fashions I do not consider solely as freaks of vanity; on the contrary, I look upon these as a ceaseless search of the human mind for the beautiful. Much less do I consider elaborate ceremony as altogether trivial; for it denotes the result of long observation as to the most appropriate method of achieving a certain result. If there is anything to do, there is certainly a best way to do it, and the best way is both the most economical and the most graceful. Mr. Spencer defines grace as the most economical manner of motion. The tea ceremony presents certain definite ways of manipulating a bowl, a spoon, a napkin, etc. To a novice it looks tedious. But one soon discovers that the way prescribed is, after all, the most saving of time and labour; in other words, the most economical use of force, — hence, according to Spencer's theory, the most graceful.

The spiritual significance of social decorum, — or, I might say, to borrow from the vocabulary of the "Philosophy of Clothes," the spiritual discipline of which etiquette and ceremony are mere outward garments, — is out of all proportion to what their appearance warrants us in believing. I might follow the example of Mr. Spencer and trace in our ceremonial institutions their origins and the moral motives that gave rise to them; but that is not what I shall endeavor to do in this book. It is the moral training involved in strict observance of propriety, that I wish to emphasize.

I have said that etiquette was elaborated into the finest niceties, so much so that different schools advocating different systems, came into existence. But they all united in the ultimate essential, and this was put by a great exponent of the best known school of etiquette, the Ogasawara, in the following terms: "The end of all etiquette is to so cultivate your mind that even when you are quietly seated, not the roughest ruffian can dare make onset on your person." It means, in other words, that by constant exercise in correct manners, one brings all the parts and faculties of his body into perfect order and into such harmony with itself and its environment as to express the mastery of spirit over the flesh. One can better appreciate the alert poise of the samurai.

If the premise is true that gracefulness means economy of force, then it follows as a logical sequence that a constant practice of graceful deportment must bring with it a reserve and storage of force. Fine manners, therefore, mean power in repose. When the barbarian Gauls, during the sack of Rome, burst into the assembled Senate and dared pull the beards of the venerable Fathers, we think the old gentlemen were to blame, inasmuch as they lacked dignity and strength of manners. Is lofty spiritual attainment really possible through etiquette? Why not? — All roads lead to Rome!

As an example of how the simplest thing can be made into an art and then become spiritual culture, I may take *Cha-no-yu*, the tea ceremony. Tea-sipping as a fine art! Why should it not be? In the children drawing pictures on the sand, or in the savage carving on a rock, was the promise of a Raphael or a Michaelangelo. How much more is the drinking of a beverage, which began with the transcendental contemplation of a Hindu anchorite, entitled to develop into a facet of Religion and Morality? That calmness of mind, that serenity of temper, that composure and quietness of demeanor which are the first essentials of *Cha-no-yu*, are without doubt the first conditions of right thinking and right feeling. The scrupulous cleanliness of the little room, shut off from sight and sound of the madding crowd, is in itself conducive to direct one's thoughts from the world. The bare interior does not engross one's attention like the innumerable pictures and bric-a-brac of a Western parlor; the presence of *kakemono** calls our attention more to grace of design than to beauty of color. The utmost refinement of taste is the object aimed at; whereas anything like display is banished with religious horror. The very fact that it was invented by a contemplative recluse, in a time when wars and the rumors of wars were incessant, is well calculated to show that this institution was more than a pastime. Before entering the quiet precincts of the tea-room, the company assembling to partake of the ceremony laid aside, together with their swords, the ferocity of battle-field or the cares of government, there to find peace and friendship.

Cha-no-yu is more than a ceremony; it is a fine art; it is poetry, with articulate gestures for rhythms: it is a *modus operandi* of soul discipline.

Politeness will be a great acquisition, if it does no more than impart grace to manners; but its function does not stop here. For propriety, springing as it does from motives of benevolence and modesty, and actuated by tender feelings toward the sensibilities of others, is ever a graceful expression of sympathy. Its require-ment is that we should weep with those that weep and rejoice with those that rejoice. Such a learned requirement, when reduced into small everyday details of life, expresses itself in little acts scarcely noticeable, or, if noticed, is, as one missionary lady of twenty years' residence once said to me, "awfully funny." You are out in the hot glaring sun with no shade over you; a Japanese acquaintance passes by; you accost him, and instantly his hat is off — well, that is perfectly natural, but the "awfully funny" performance is, that all the while he talks with you his parasol is down and he stands in the glaring sun also. How foolish! — Yes, exactly so, provided the motive were less than this: "You are in the sun; I sympathize with you; I would willingly take you under

*Hanging scrolls, which may be either paintings or ideograms, used for decorative purposes.

my parasol if it were large enough, or if we were familiarly acquainted; as I cannot shade you, I will share your discomforts." Little acts of this kind, equally or more amusing, are not mere gestures or conventionalities. They are the "bodying forth" of thoughtful feelings for the comfort of others.

Another "awfully funny" custom is dictated by our canons of Politeness; but many thoughtless writers on Japan have dismissed it by simply attributing it to the general topsy-turveyness of the nation. Every foreigner who has observed it will confer the awkwardness he felt in making proper reply upon the occasion. In America, when you make a gift, you sing its praises to the recipient; in Japan we depreciate or slander it. The underlying idea with you is, "This is a nice gift: if it were not nice I would not dare give it to you; for it will be an insult to give you anything but what is nice." In contrast to this, our logic runs: "You are a nice person, and no gift is nice enough for you. You will not accept anything I can lay at your feet except as a token of my good will; so accept this, not for its intrinsic value, but as a token. It will be an insult to your worth to call the best gift good enough for you." Place the two ideas side by side, and we see that the ultimate idea is one and the same. Neither is "awfully funny." The American speaks of the material which makes the gift; the Japanese speaks of the spirit that prompts the gift.

It is perverse reasoning to conclude, because our sense of propriety shows itself in all the smallest ramifications of our deportment, to take the least important of them and uphold it as the type, and pass judgment upon the principle itself. Which is more important, to eat or to observe rules of propriety about eating? A Chinese sage answers, "If you take a case where the eating is all-important, and the observing the rules of propriety is of little importance, and compare them together, why merely say that the eating is of the more importance?" "Metal is heavier than feathers," but does that saying have reference to a single clasp of metal and a wagon-load of feathers? Take a piece of wood a foot thick and raise it above the pinnacle of a temple, none would call it taller than the temple. To the question, "Which is the more important, to tell the truth or to be polite?" the Japanese are said to give an answer diametrically opposite to what the American will say.

... the word of a samurai was sufficient guarantee for the truthfulness of an assertion.

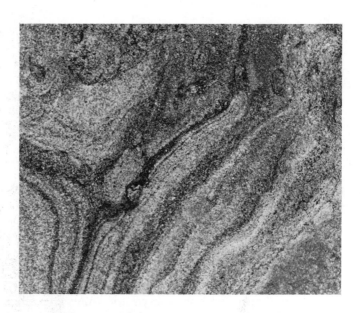

Veracity

Probing the field of veracity leads one into a bog of enigmas. According to the code of Bushido, lying was deemed cowardly. As such it was regarded as dishonorable. Indeed, the word of a samurai guaranteed the truthfulness of an assertion. Usually no oath was necessary. The samurai never swore an oath on the Bible as Westerners are often required to do. They did add some weight to their word by sometimes swearing on their sword or to some deity. But a formal oath was regarded as derogatory to a samurai's personal word of honor.

Would the samurai be impolite or would he tell a falsehood? According to Masamune, "Propriety carried beyond bounds becomes a lie."

The samurai had a neat definition of falsehood. The word uso, anything not a makoto (truth) or a honto (fact), left him room to be somewhat elastic in his concept of veracity. He might slide by the point of absolute truth. His sense of courtesy might demand that he do so. It simply meant that he stretched both veracity and politeness. But even today, those who strive to live by the code of Bushido strive for honesty.

When the age of feudalism ended, the samurai class entered commerce. There they discovered that the merchant class was not bound by the code of Bushido. When the country opened to foreign trade only the most adventurous and unscrupulous rushed *to the treaty ports to do business. Lacking in shrewdness most samurai did not survive for very long in the business world. They discovered that veracity had almost no meaning in industry, very little in the field of politics and a great deal of meaning only in the world of philosophy—their world.*

Veracity was an extension of the samurai's vision of courage. As such he blended it with honor.

VERACITY OR TRUTHFULNESS

Without veracity politeness is a farce. "Propriety carried beyond right bounds," says Masamuné, "becomes a lie." An ancient poet has outdone Polonius in the advice he gives: "To thyself be faithful: if in thy heart thou strayest not from truth, without prayer of thine the Gods will keep thee whole."

Lying or equivocation were deemed equally cowardly. The bushi held that his high social position demanded a loftier standard of veracity than that of the tradesman and peasant. *Bushi-no ichi-gon* — the word of a samurai — was sufficient guarantee for the truthfulness of an assertion. His word carried such weight with it that promises were generally made and fulfilled without a written pledge, which would have been deemed quite beneath his dignity. Many thrilling anecdotes were told of those who atoned by death for *ni-gon*, a double tongue.

The regard for veracity was so high that, unlike the generality of Christians who persistently violate the plain commands of the Teacher not to swear, the best of samurai looked upon an oath as derogatory to their honor. I am well aware that they did swear by different deities or upon their swords; but never has swearing degenerated into wanton form and irreverent interjection. To emphasize our words a practice of literally sealing with blood was sometimes resorted to. For the explanation of such a practice, I need only refer my readers to Goethe's Faust.

A recent American writer is responsible for this statement, that if you ask an ordinary Japanese which is better, to tell a falsehood or be impolite, he will not hesitate to answer "to tell a falsehood!" Dr. Peery* is partly right and partly wrong; right in that an ordinary Japanese, even a samurai, may answer in the way ascribed

*Peery, The Gist of Japan, p. 86.

to him, but wrong in attributing too much weight to the term he translates "falsehood." This word (in Japanese *uso*) is employed to denote anything which is not a truth (makoto) or fact (honto). Lowell tells us that Wordsworth could not distinguish between truth and fact, and an ordinary Japanese is in this respect as good as Wordsworth. Ask a Japanese, or even an American of any refinement, to tell you whether he dislikes you or whether he is sick at his stomach, and he will not hesitate long to tell falsehoods and answer "I like you much," or, "I am quite well, thank you." To sacrifice truth for the sake of politeness was regarded as an "empty form" *(kyo-ré)* and deception by sweet words."

I own I am speaking now of the Bushido idea of veracity: but it may not be amiss to devote a few words to our commercial integrity, of which I have heard much complaint in foreign books and journals. A loose business morality has indeed been the worst blot on our national reputation; but before abusing it or hastily condemning the whole race for it, let us calmly study it and we shall be rewarded with consolation for the future.

Of all the great occupations of life, none was farther removed from the profession of arms than commerce. The merchant was placed lowest in the category of vocations, — the knight, the tiller of the soil, the mechanic, the merchant. The samurai derived his income from land and could even indulge, if he had a mind to, in amateur farming; but the counter and abacus were abhorred. We know the wisdom of this social arrangement. Montesquieu has made it clear that the debarring of the nobility from mercantile pursuits was an admirable social policy, in that it prevented wealth from accumulating in the hands of the powerful. The separation of power and riches kept the distribution of the latter more nearly equable. Professor Dill, the author of "Roman Society in the Last Century of the Western Empire," has brought afresh to our mind that one cause of the decadence of the Roman Empire, was the permission given to the nobility to engage in trade, and the consequent monopoly of wealth and power by a minority of the senatorial families.

Commerce, therefore, in feudal Japan did not reach the degree of development which it would have attained under freer conditions. The obloquy attached to the calling naturally brought within its pale such as cared little for social repute. "Call one a thief and he will steal." Put a stigma on a calling and its followers adjust their morals to it. It is unnecessary to add that no business commercial or otherwise, can be transacted without a code of morals. Our merchants of the feudal period had one among themselves, without which they could never have developed, as they did, such fundamental mercantile institutions as the guild, the bank, the bourse, insurance, checks, bills of exchange, etc.; but in their relations with people outside their vocation, the tradesmen lived too true to the reputation of their order.

This being the case, when the country was opened to foreign trade, only the most adventurous and unscrupulous rushed to the ports, while the respectable business houses declined for some time the repeated requests of the authorities to establish branch houses. Was Bushido powerless to stay the current of commercial dishonor? Let us see.

Those who are well acquainted with our history will remember that only a few years after our treaty ports were opened to foreign trade, feudalism was abolished, and when with it the samurai's fiefs were taken and bonds issued to them in compensation, they were given liberty to invest them in mercantile transactions. Now you may ask, "Why could they not bring their much boasted veracity into new business relations and so reform the old abuses?" Those who had eyes to see could not weep enough, those who had hearts to feel could not sympathize enough, with the fate of many a noble and honest samurai who signally and irrevocably failed in his new and unfamiliar field of trade and industry, through sheer lack of shrewdness in coping with his artful plebeian rival. When we know that eighty per cent of the business houses fail in so industrial a country as America, is it any wonder that scarcely one among a hundred samurai who went into trade could succeed in his new vocation? It will be long before it will be recognized how many fortunes were wrecked in the attempt to apply Bushido ethics to business methods; but it was soon patent to every observing mind that the ways of wealth were not the ways of honor. In what respects, then, were they different?

Of the three incentives to Veracity that Lecky enumerates, viz: the industrial, the political, and the philosophical, the first was altogether lacking in Bushido. As to the second, it could develop little in a political community under feudal system. It is in its philosophical, and as Lecky says, in its highest aspect, that Honesty attained elevated rank in our catalogue of virtues. With all my sincere regard for the high commercial integrity of the Anglo-Saxon race, when I ask for the ultimate ground, I am told that "Honesty is the best policy," — that it *pays* to be honest. Is not this virtue, then, its own reward? If it is followed because it brings in more cash than falsehood, I am afraid Bushido will rather indulge in lies!

If Bushido rejects a doctrine like this, the shrewder tradesman will readily accept it. Lecky has very truly remarked that Veracity owes its growth largely to commerce and manufacture, — in other words, that it is the foster-child of industry. Without this mother, Veracity was like a blue-blood orphan whom only the most cultivated mind could adopt and nourish. Such minds were general among the samurai, but, for want of a more democratic and utilitarian foster-mother, the tender child failed to thrive. Industries advancing, Veracity will prove an easy, nay, a profitable, virtue to practice. Already our merchants have found that out. For the rest I recommend the reader to two recent writers for well-weighted judgment on this point.* It is interesting to remark in this connection that integrity and honor were the surest guarantees which even a merchant debtor could present in the form of promissory notes. It was quite a usual thing to insert such clauses as these: "In default of the re-payment of the sum lent to me, I shall say nothing against being ridiculed in public;" or, "In case I fail to pay you back, you may call me a fool," and the like.

Often have I wondered whether the Veracity of Bushido had any motive higher than courage. In the absence of any positive commandment against bearing false witness, lying was not condemned as sin, but simply denounced as weakness, and, as such, highly dishonorable.

*Knapp, Feudal and Modern Japan, Vol. I, Ch. iv.
*Ransome, Japan in Transition, Ch. viii.

. . . dishonor is like a scar on a tree, which time, instead of effacing, only helps to enlarge."

Honor

A vivid consciousness of personal dignity and worth is implicit in the word honor. Honor was conveyed by such terms as na *(name),* men-moku *and* guai bun *(external bearing). Any infringement upon a samurai's honor was felt as* ren-chi-shin *(a sense of shame).*

The young novice was often asked, "Are you not ashamed?" The sense of shame was regarded as one of the earliest indications of moral consciousness. Disobedience to a code or to a superior produced feelings of guilt and shame.

According to a samurai legend, "Dishonor is like a scar on a tree, which time, instead of effacing only helps to enlarge."

In the name of honor, deeds were perpetrated which can find no justification in the code of Bushido. Legends lead us to believe that tales of vengence for even an imaginary slur on samurai honor produced brutal results. It is clear that many of the tales are false. They were used to overawe the general public. Sometimes they did set straight apparent abuses to a samurai's honor. Mostly they served to prove that the samurai had an extremely strong sense of shame.

To avoid excessive over-reacting to small slights the samurai chided each other for being too short-tempered. They also comforted themselves with the adage, "To bear what you think you cannot bear is really to bear." Patience and forgiveness formed an essential part of the meaning of honor.

Life was thought cheap if honor and fame could be had by giving it up. But if a cause presented itself that was deemed dearer than life, with serenity and speed life was ended.

HONOR

The sense of honor, implying a vivid consciousness of personal dignity and worth, could not fail to characterize the samurai, born and bred to value the duties and privileges of their profession. Though the word ordinarily given now-a-days as the translation of Honor was not used freely, yet the idea was conveyed by such terms as *na* (name) *men-moku* (countenance), *guai bun* (outside bearing), reminding us respectively of the biblical use of "name," of the evolution of the term "personality" from the Greek mask, and of "fame." A good name being assumed as a matter of course, any infringement upon its integrity was felt as shame, and the sense of shame *(Ren-chi-shin)* was one of the earliest to be cherished in juvenile education. "You will be laughed at," "It will disgrace you," "Are you not ashamed?" were the last appeal to correct behavior on the part of a youthful delinquent. Such a recourse to his honor touched the most sensitive spot in the child's heart, as though it had been nursed on honor while it was in its mother's womb. Indeed, the sense of shame seems to me to be the earliest indication of moral consciousness. The first and worst punishment which befell humanity in consequence of tasting "the fruit of that forbidden tree" was, to my mind, not the sorrow of childbirth, nor the thorns and thistles, but the awakening of the sense of shame. Few incidents in history excel in pathos the scene of the first mother plying, with heaving breast and tremulous fingers, her crude needle on the few fig leaves which her dejected husband plucked for her. This first fruit of disobedience clings to us with a tenacity that nothing else does. All the sartorial ingenuity of mankind has not yet succeeded in sewing an apron that will effectively hide our

sense of shame. That samurai was right who refused to com-
promise his character by a slight humiliation in his youth;
"because," he said, "dishonor is like a scar on a tree, which time,
instead of effacing, only helps to enlarge."

Mencius had taught centuries before, in almost the identical
phrase, what Carlyle has latterly expressed, — namely, that
"Shame is the soil of all Virtue, of good manners and good
morals."

The fear of disgrace was so great that if our literature lacks such
eloquence as Shakespeare puts into the mouth of Norfolk, it
nevertheless hung like Damocles' sword over the head of every
samurai and often assumed a morbid character. In the name of
Honor, deeds were perpetrated which can find no justification in
the code of Bushido. At the slightest, or even imagined insult, the
quick-tempered braggart took offense, resorted to the use of the
sword, and many unnecessary fights were started and many
innocent lives lost. The story of a well-meaning citizen who called
the attention of a bushi to a flea jumping on his back, and who
was forthwith cut in two, for the simple and questionable reason
that inasmuch as fleas are parasites which feed on animals, it was
an unpardonable insult to identify a noble warrior with a beast — I
say, stories like these are too frivolous to believe. Yet, the
circulation of such stories implies three things; (1) that they were
invented to overawe common people; (2) that abuses were really
made of the samurai's profession of honor; and (3) that a very
strong sense of shame was developed among them. It is plainly
unfair to take an abnormal case to cast blame upon the Precepts,
any more than to judge of the true teachings of Christ from the
fruits of religious fanaticism and extravagance — inquisitions and
hypocrisy. But, as in religious monomania there is something
touchingly noble, as compared with the delirium tremens of a
drunkard, so in that extreme sensitiveness of the samurai about
their honor do we not recognize the substratum of a genuine
virtue?

The morbid excess into which the delicate code of honor was
inclined to run was strongly counter-balanced by preaching
magnanimity and patience. To take offense at slight provocation
was ridiculed as "short-tempered." The popular adage said: "To
bear what you think you cannot bear is really to bear." The great
Iyéyasu left to posterity a few maxims, among which are the
following: — "The life of man is like going a long distance with a

heavy load upon the shoulders. Haste not.* * * * * Reproach none, but be forever watchful of thine own short-comings.* * * * Forbearance is the basis of length of days." He proved in his life what he preached. A literary wit put a characteristic epigram into the mouths of three well-known personages in our history: to Nobunaga he attributed, "I will kill her if the nightingale sings not in time;" to Hidéyoshi, "I will force her to sing for me;" and to Iyéyasu, "I will wait till she opens her lips."

Patience and long suffering were also highly commended by Mencius. In one place he writes to this effect: "Though you denude yourself and insult me, what is that to me? You cannot defile my soul by your outrage." Elsewhere he teaches that anger at a petty offense is unworthy a superior man, but indignation for a great cause is righteous wrath.

To what height of unmartial and unresisting meekness Bushido could reach in some of its votaries, may be seen in their utterances. Take, for instance, this saying of Ogawa: "When others speak all manner of evil things against you, return not evil for evil, but rather reflect that you were not more faithful in the discharge of your duties." Take another of Kumazawa: — "When others blame you, blame them not; when others are angry at you, return not anger. Joy comes only as Passion and Desire part." Still another instance I may cite from Saigo: "The Way is the way of Heaven and Earth: Man's place is to follow it: therefore make it the object of your life to reverence Heaven. Heaven loves me and others with equal love; therefore with the love wherewith you love yourself, love others. Make not Man your partner but Heaven, and making Heaven your partner do your best. Never condemn others; but see to it that you come not short of your own mark." Some of these sayings remind us of Christian expostulations and show us how far in practical morality natural religion can approach the revealed. Not only did these sayings remain as utterances, but they were really embodied in acts.

It must be admitted that very few attained this sublime height of magnanimity, patience and forgiveness. It was a great pity that nothing clear and general was expressed as to what constitutes Honor, only a few enlightened minds being aware that it "from no condition rises," but that it lies in each acting well his part. For the most part, an insult was quickly resented and repaid by death, as we shall see later, while Honor — too often nothing higher than worldly approbation — was prized as the *summum bonum* of earthly existence. Fame, and not wealth or knowledge, was the goal toward which youths had to strive. Many a lad swore within himself as he crossed the threshold of his paternal home, that he would not recross it until he had made a name in the world: and many an ambitious mother refused to see her darling again unless he could "return home," as the expression is, "caparisoned in brocade." To shun shame or win a name, samurai boys would submit to any privations and undergo severest ordeals of bodily or mental suffering. Life itself was thought cheap if honor and fame could be purchased therewith: hence, whenever a cause presented itself which was considered dearer than life, with utmost serenity and speed life was laid down.

. . . Loyalty as we conceive it may find few admirers elsewhere, not because our conception is wrong, but because it is, I am afraid, forgotten . . .

The Duty of Loyalty

Only in the code of chivalrous honor does loyalty assume importance. Loyalty to the state or to one's feudal lord were the most important aspects of this trait. Establishment of personal loyalty to the Emperor was deemed "excellent within certain bounds."

In China, Confucian ethics made obedience and loyalty to parents the primary human duty; in Japan precedence was given to loyalty to the state as embodied in the Emperor.

In the conflict between loyalty or affection, the code of Bushido never wavered from the choice of loyalty.

School children were taught to sacrifice everything for the Emperor. A loyal mother stood ready to sacrifice her sons in the cause of loyalty. This ingrained attitude lead to absolutism and despotism. It was similar to the feudal states of Europe. When Frederick the Great of Prussia said, "Kings are the first servants of the State," he ushered in a new era in the development of freedom. Simultaneously in the backwoods of Northern Japan, Yozan of Yonezawa made the same declaration.

A feudal lord, unmindful of a sense of obligation to his vassals, felt a sense of responsibility to his ancestors and to the Emperor. He was obliged to act as a father to his subjects, to guard their welfare. The Spanish system of encomienda established in 1503 for colonization of New Spain was almost identical.

Both the Bushido and Aristotelian philosophies regarded the state as predating the individual. A person was born into the state.

He was obliged to live and die for it, or for the symbol of its legitimate authority. In Japan, the laws and the state were represented by a personal being, the Emperor. Loyalty was an ethical demand stemming from this political theory.

For a time, Christianity was suppressed because it was thought no one could serve two masters—God and the Emperor. When the persecution of the Christians ran its course it was decided that it was indeed possible to "serve two masters without holding to the one and despising the other." This concept was strikingly similar to the Biblical admonition to "render unto Caesar the things that are Caesar's and unto God the things that are God's."

A man could not sacrifice his own conscience to the capricious will or freak fancy of a sovereign. Such a one was to be despised as nei-chin *(a cringling) or a* cho-shin *(a sycophant) who stole his master's affection by unscrupulous fawning and servile compliance.*

A samurai was obliged to appeal to the intelligence and conscience of his sovereign by demonstrating the sincerity of his words with the shedding of his own blood.

THE DUTY OF LOYALTY

Loyalty was the key-stone making feudal virtues a symmetrical arch. Other virtues feudal morality shares in common with other systems of ethics, with other classes of people, but this virtue — homage and fealty to a superior — is its distinctive feature. I am aware that personal fidelity is moral adhesion existing among all sorts and conditions of men, — a gang of pick-pockets owe allegiance to a Fagin; but it is only in the code of chivalrous honor that Loyalty assumes paramount importance.

In spite of Hegel's criticism* that the fidelity of feudal vassals, being an obligation to an individual and not to a Commonwealth, is a bond established on totally unjust principles, a great compatriot of his made it his boast that personal loyalty was a German virtue. Bismarck had good reasons to do so, not because the *Treue* he boasts of was the monopoly of his Fatherland or of any single nation or race, but because this favored fruit of chivalry lingers latest among the people where feudalism lasted longest. In

*Philosophy of History (Eng. trans. by Sibree), Pt. IV., Sec. ii, Ch. I.

America where "everybody is as good as anybody else," and, as the Irishman added, "better too," such exalted ideas of loyalty as we feel for our sovereign may be deemed "excellent within certain bounds," but preposterous as encouraged among us. Montesquieu complained long ago that right on one side of the Pyrenees was wrong on the other, and the Dreyfus trials proved the truth of his remark, save that the Pyrenees were not the sole boundary beyond which French justice finds no accord. Similarly, Loyalty as we conceive it may find few admirers elsewhere, not because our conception is wrong, but because it is, I am afraid, forgotten, and also because we carry it to a degree not reached in any other country. Griffis* was quite right in stating that whereas in China Confucian ethics made obedience to parents the primary human duty, in Japan precedence was given to Loyalty. At the risk of shocking some of my good readers, I will cite one out of innumerable examples of Loyalty, as it is an instance well-known in our literature.

The story is one of the greatest characters of our history, Michizané, who, falling a victim to jealousy and calumny, is exiled from the capital. Not content with this, his unrelenting enemies are now bent upon the extinction of his family. Strict search for his son — not yet grown — reveals the fact of his being secreted in a village school kept by one Genzo, a former vassal of Michizané. When orders are dispatched to the schoolmaster to deliver the head of the juvenile offender on a certain day, his first idea is to find a suitable substitute for it. He ponders over his school-list, scrutinizes with careful eyes all the boys, as they stroll into the class-room, but none among the children born of the soil bears the least resemblance to his protégé. His despair, however, is but for a moment; for, behold, a new scholar is announced — a comely boy of the same age as his master's son, escorted by a mother of noble mien. Here, then, is the scapegoat! — The rest of the narrative may be briefly told. — On the day appointed arrives the officer commissioned to identify and receive the head of the youth. Will he be deceived by the false head? The poor Genzo's hand is on the hilt of the sword, ready to strike a blow either at the man or at himself, should the examination defeat his scheme. The officer takes up the gruesome object before him, goes calmly over each feature, and in a deliberate, business-like tone, pronounces it

*Religions of Japan.

genuine. — That evening in a lonely home awaits the mother we saw in the school. Does she know the fate of her darling? It is not for his return that she watches with eagerness for the opening of the wicket. Her father-in-law has been for a long time a recipient of Michizané's bounties, and after his banishment her husband continued in the service of the enemy of his family benefactor. He himself could not be untrue to his own cruel master; but his son could serve the cause of the grandsire's lord. As one acquainted with the exile's family, he was entrusted with the task of identifying the boy's head. Now the day's — yea, the life's — hard work is done, he returns home and as he crosses its threshold, he accosts his wife, saying: "Rejoice, my wife, our darling son has proved of service to his lord!"

"What an atrocious story!" I hear my readers exclaim. "Parents deliberately sacrificing their own innocent child to save the life of another man's." But this child was a conscious and willing victim: it is a story of vicarious death — as significant and not more revolting than the story of Abraham's intended sacrifice of Isaac. In both cases it was obedience to the call of duty.

The individualism of the West, which recognizes separate interests for father and son, husband and wife, necessarily brings into strong relief the duties owed by one to the other; but Bushido held that the interest of the family and of the members thereof is intact, — one and inseparable. This interest it wound up with affection — natural, instinctive, irresistible; hence, if we die for one we love with natural love (which animals themselves possess), what is that? "For if ye love them that love you, what reward have ye? Do not even the publicans the same?"

In his great history, Sanyo relates in touching language the heart struggle of Shigemori concerning his father's rebellious conduct. "If I be loyal, my father must be undone; if I obey my father, my duty to my sovereign must go amiss." Poor Shigemori! We see him afterward praying with all his soul that kind Heaven may visit him with death, that he may be released from this world where it is hard for purity and righteousness to dwell.

Many a Shigemori has his heart torn by the conflict between duty and affection. In such conflicts Bushido never wavered in its choice of Loyalty. Women, too, encouraged their offspring to sacrifice all for the king. Even as resolute as Widow Windham and her illustrious consort, the samurai matron stood ready to give up her boys for the cause of Loyalty. An utter surrender of "life and limb" on the part of the governed, left nothing for the governing but self-will, and this has for its natural consequence the growth of that absolutism so often called "oriental despotism," as though there were no despots of occidental history!

Let it be far from me to uphold despotism of any sort; but it is a mistake to identify feudalism with it. When Frederick the Great wrote that "Kings are the first servants of the State," jurists thought rightly that a new era was reached in the development of freedom. Strangely coinciding in time, in the backwoods of Northwestern Japan, Yozan of Yonézawa made exactly the same declaration, showing that feudalism was not all tyranny and oppression. "Absolutism" says Bismarck, "primarily demands impartiality, honesty, devotion to duty, energy and inward humility in the ruler." A feudal prince, although unmindful of owing reciprocal obligations to his vassals, felt a higher sense of responsibility to his ancestors and to Heaven. He was a father to his subjects, whom Heaven entrusted to his care. In a sense not usually assigned to the term, Bushido accepted and corroborated paternal government — paternal also as opposed to the less interested avuncular government (Uncle Sam's, to wit!). The difference between a despotic and a paternal government lies in this, that in the one the people obey reluctantly, while in the other they do so with "that proud submission, that dignified obedience, that subordination of heart which kept alive, even in servitude itself, the spirit of exalted freedom."* The old saying is not entirely false which called the king of England the "king of devils, because of his subjects' often insurrections against, and depositions of, their princes," and which made the French monarch the "king of asses," "because of their infinite taxes and impositions," but which gave the title of the king of men to the sovereign of Spain "because of his subjects' willing obedience." But enough!—

Since Bushido, like Aristotle and some modern sociologists, conceived the state as antedating the individual, — the latter being born into the former as part and parcel thereof — he must live and die for it or for the incumbent of its legitimate authority. In Bushido the laws and the state were represented with us by a personal being. Loyalty is an ethical outcome of this political theory.

*Burke, French Revolution.

I am not entirely ignorant of Mr. Spencer's view according to which political obedience — Loyalty — is accredited with only a transitional function.* It may be so. We may complacently repeat it, especially as we believe *that* day to be a long space of time, during which, so our national anthem says, "tiny pebbles grow into mighty rocks draped with moss."

Political subordination, Mr. Spencer predicts, will give place to loyalty, to the dictates of conscience. Suppose his induction is realized — will loyalty and its concomitant instinct of reverence disappear forever? We transfer our allegiance from one master to another, without being unfaithful to either: from being subjects of a ruler that wields the temporal sceptre we become servants of the monarch who sits enthroned in the penetralia of our heart. A few years ago a very stupid controversy started by the misguided disciples of Spencer, made havoc among the reading class of Japan. In their zeal to uphold the claim of the throne to undivided loyalty, they charged Christians with treasonable propensity in that they avow fidelity to their Lord and Master. They arrayed forth sophistical arguments without the wit of Sophists, and scholastic tortuosities minus the niceties of the Schoolmen. Little did they know that we can, in a sense, "serve two masters without holding to the one or despising the other," "rendering unto Caesar the things that are Caesar's and unto God the things that are God's." Did not Socrates, all the while he unflinchingly refused to concede one iota of loyalty to his *daemon*, obey with equal fidelity and equanimity the command of his early master, the State?

Bushido did not require us to make our conscience the slave of any lord or king. Thomas Mowbray was a veritable spokesman for us when he said: —

> "Myself I throw, dread sovereign, at thy foot.
> My life thou shall command, but not my shame.
> The one my duty owes; but my fair name,
> Despite of death, that lives upon my grave,
> To dark dishonor's use, thou shall not have."

A man who sacrificed his own conscience to the capricious will or freak or fancy of a sovereign was accorded a low place in the estimate of the Precepts. Such a one was despised as *nei-shin*, a cringling, who makes court by unscrupulous fawning, or as *chô-shin*, a favorite who steals his master's affections by means of

*Principles of Ethics, Vol. I, Pt. II, Ch. x.

servile compliance. When a subject differed from his master, the loyal path for him to pursue was to use every available means to persuade him of his error, as Kent did to King Lear. Failing in this, let the master deal with him as he wills. In cases of this kind, it was quite a usual course for the samurai to make the last appeal to the intelligence and conscience of his lord by demonstrating the sincerity of his words with the shedding of his own blood.

Life being regarded as the means whereby to serve his master, and its ideal being set upon honor, the whole training of a samurai was conducted accordingly.

. . . it was with a practical end in view that education was conducted.

Education and Training of a Samurai

The basic framework of Bushido consists of chi *(wisdom),* jin *(benevolence) and* yu *(courage).*

A samurai was essentially a man of action. Science was not included in the scope of his activities. Religion and theology were relegated to the priests. The samurai used them only to nourish his courage. "Tis not the creed that saves the man, but it is the man that justifies the creed." He studied philosophy and literature, but he did not strive for objective truth. Philosophy was used as an aid in forming his character, and it occasionally served in the solution of a political or military problem. It was the perfect method for rationalization. Literature was regarded as a worthy pastime.

The main points in the curriculum of Bushido were fencing, archery, horsemanship, use of the spear, tactics, ethics, literature, history, calligraphy and jiu-jutsu. In the study of jiu-jutsu the samurai was not to maim or kill his opponent; he was only to put him out of commission or action for the time being. The rigorous study of the martial arts included combinations from all of these arts.

Mathematics was not taught. Feudal warfare was waged without scientific precision. Counting of money was deemed a task too menial for the samurai. Ignorance of the value of coins was a token of good breeding. Thrift was practiced as an exercise in abstinence, not for economy.

By and large the samurai studied literature and moral obligations to teach him to reach rapidly the essential decisions of character.

The samurai followed the teaching of Confucius, "Learning without thought is labor lost; thought without learning is perilous." Development of character and soul was regarded as a sacred trust that teachers were obliged to bestow upon their students. "It is the parent who has borne me. It is the teacher who makes me man," was a basic axiom in the development of a samurai.

Payment for services was demeaning. How could one pay for an invaluable service? It was really thought to be impossible. But periodically they presented offerings of money or goods to their teachers as a token of gratitude and esteem. The teachers were stern and honorable men, boasting of dignified penury, too proud to work with their hands and above begging. They personified high spirits undaunted by adversity. They were the living embodiments of discipline.

EDUCATION AND TRAINING OF A SAMURAI

The first point to observe in knightly training was to build up character, leaving in the shade the subtler faculties of prudence, intelligence and logical debate. We have seen the important part aesthetic accomplishments played in his education. Indispensable as they were to a man of culture, they were accessories rather than essentials of samurai training. Intellectual superiority was, of course, esteemed: but the word *Chi*, which was employed to denote intellectuality, meant wisdom in the first instance and placed knowledge only in a very subordinate place. The tripod that supported the framework of Bushido was said to be *Chi, Jin, Yu*, respectively Wisdom, Benevolence, and Courage. A samurai was essentially a man of action. Science was out of the pale of his activity. He took advantage of it in so far as it concerned his profession of arms. Religion and theology were relegated to the priests; he concerned himself with them in so far as they helped to nourish courage. Like an English poet the samurai believed " 'tis not the creed that saves the man; but it is the man that justifies the creed." Philosophy and literature formed the chief part of his intellectual training; but even in the pursuit of these, it was not objective truth that he strove after, — literature was pursued mainly as a pastime, and philosophy as a practical aid in the formation of character, if not for the exposition of some military or political problem.

From what has been said, it will not be surprising to note that the curriculum of studies, according to the pedagogics of Bushido, consisted mainly of the following, — fencing, archery, *jiu-jutsu* or *yawara*, horsemanship, the use of the spear, tactics, calligraphy, ethics, literature and history. Of these, *jiu-jutsu* and calligraphy may require a few words of explanation. Great stress was laid on good writing, probably because our logograms, partaking as they do of the nature of pictures, possess artistic value, and also because chirography was accepted as indicative of one's personal character. *Jiu-jutsu* may be briefly defined as an application of anatomical knowledge to the purpose of offense or defense. It differs from wrestling, in that it does not depend upon muscular strength. It differs from other forms of attack in that it uses no weapon. Its feat consists in clutching or striking such part of the enemy's body as will make him numb and incapable of resistance. Its object is not to kill, but to incapacitate one for action for the time being.

A subject of study which one would expect to find in military education and which is rather conspicuous by its absence in the Bushido course of instruction, is mathematics. This, however, can be readily explained in part by the fact that feudal warfare was not carried on with scientific precision. Not only that, but the whole training of the samurai was unfavorable to fostering numerical notions.

Chivalry is uneconomical; it boasts in penury. Don Quixote takes more pride in his rusty spear and skin-and-bone horse than in gold and lands, and a samurai is in hearty sympathy with his exaggerated confrére of La Mancha. He disdains money itself, — the art of making or hoarding it. It was to him veritably filthy lucre. "Less than all things," says a current precept, "men must grudge money; it is by riches that wisdom is hindered." Hence children were brought up with utter disregard of economy. It was considered bad taste to speak of it, and ignorance of the value of different coins was a token of good breeding. Knowledge of numbers was indispensable in the mustering of forces as well as in distribution of benefices and fiefs; but the counting of money was left to meaner hands. In many feudatories, public finance was administered by a lower kind of samurai or by priests. Every thinking bushi knew well enough that money formed the sinews of war; but he did not think of raising the appreciation of money to a virtue. It is true that thrift was enjoined by Bushido, but not for economical reasons so much as for the exercise of abstinence.

We read that in ancient Rome the farmers of revenue and other financial agents were gradually raised to the rank of knights, the State thereby showing its appreciation of their service and of the importance of money itself. How closely this is connected with the luxury and avarice of the Romans may be imagined. Not so with the Precepts of Knighthood. It persisted in systematically regarding finance as something low — low as compared with moral and intellectual vocations.

Money and the love of it being thus diligently ignored, Bushido itself could long remain free from a thousand and one evils of which money is the root.

The mental discipline which would now-a-days be chiefly aided by the study of mathematics, was supplied by literary explanations and studies of moral obligations. Very few abstract subjects troubled the mind of the young, the chief aim of their education being, as I have said, decision of character. People whose minds were simply stored with information found no great admirers. Of the three services of studies that Bacon gives, — for delight, ornament, and ability, — Bushido had decided preference for the last, where their use was "in judgment and the disposition of business." Whether it was for the disposition of public business or for the exercise of self-control, it was with a practical end in view that education was conducted. "Learning without thought," said Confucius, "is labor lost: thought without learning is perilous."

When character and not intelligence, when the soul and not the head, is chosen by a teacher for the material to work upon and to develop, his vocation partakes of a sacred character. "It is the parent who has borne me: it is the teacher who makes me man." With this idea, therefore, the esteem in which one's master or tutor was held was very high. A man to evoke such confidence and respect from the young, must necessarily be endowed with superior personality without lacking erudition. He was a father to the fatherless, and an adviser to the erring. "Thy father and thy mother" — so runs our maxim — "are like heaven and earth: thy teacher and thy lord are like the sun and moon."

The modern system of paying for every sort of service was not in vogue among the adherents of Bushido. It believed in a service which can be rendered only without money and without price. Spiritual service, be it of priest or teacher, was not to be repaid in gold or silver, not because it was valueless but because it was invaluable. Here the non-arithmetical honor-instinct of Bushido taught a truer lesson than modern Political Economy; for wages and salaries can be paid only for services whose results are definite, tangible, and measurable, whereas the best service done in education, — namely, in soul development (and this includes the services of a pastor), is not definite, tangible or measurable. Being immeasurable, money, the ostensible measure of value, is of inadequate use. Usage sanctioned that pupils brought to their teachers money or goods at different seasons of the year; but these were not payments but offerings, which indeed were welcome to the recipients as they were usually men of stern calibre, boasting of honorable penury, too dignified to work with their hands and too proud to beg. They were grave personifications of high spirits undaunted by adversity. They were an embodiment of what was considered as an end of all learning, and were thus a living example of that discipline of disciplines, self-control a universal requirement of the samurai.

"He shows no sign of joy or anger."

Self-Control

Fortitude, endurance and politeness required samurai to avoid marring the pleasure or security of others by expressing sorrow or pain. Development of these disciplines engendered a stoical state of mind. In view of the persistent trait of tenderness stoicism appears to be an enigma.

This enigma appears to pose the question as to whether

stoicisim steels the nerves or makes the stoic a more sensitive person.

It was unmanly for a samurai to betray his emotions on his face. "He shows no sign of joy or anger," described one of great character.

As an escape valve for suppressed feelings the samurai were encouraged to write poetry that took a rather formal style but contained rather earthy adages such as . . . "Humanity, when moved by sorrow, tells its bitter grief in verse." In Japanese calligraphy and in the spoken meter of the line, this was calculated to have a sharp impact.

Throughout the world the characteristic of self-restraint has produced a stereotype of the stoic. In reality, stoicism only masks excitability and sensitiveness.

Long years of discipline and self-repression are believed to have created a fertile field for institutionalizing self-destructive tendencies thought essential to regain honor.

SELF-CONTROL

The discipline of fortitude on the one hand, inculcating endurance without a groan, and the teaching of politeness on the other, requiring us not to mar the pleasure or serenity of another by expressions of our own sorrow or pain, combined to engender a stoical turn of mind, and eventually to confirm it into a national trait of apparent stoicism. I say apparent stoicism, because I do not believe that true stoicism can ever become the characteristic of a whole nation, and also because some of our national manners and customs may seem to a foreign observer hard-hearted. Yet we are really as susceptible to tender emotion as any race under the sky.

I am inclined to think that in one sense we have to feel more than others — yes, doubly more — since the very attempt to restrain natural promptings entails suffering. Imagine boys — and girls too — brought up not to resort to the shedding of a tear or the uttering of a groan for the relief of their feelings, — and there is a physiological problem whether such effort steels their nerves or makes them more sensitive.

It was considered unmanly for a samurai to betray his emotions on his face. "He shows no sign of joy or anger," was a phrase used in describing a great character. The most natural affections were kept under control. A father could embrace his son only at the expense of his dignity; a husband would not kiss his wife, — no, not in the presence of other people, whatever he may do in private! There may be some truth in the remark of a witty youth when he said, "American husbands kiss their wives in public and beat them in private; Japanese husbands beat theirs in public and kiss them in private."

Calmness of behavior, composure of mind, should not be disturbed by passion of any kind. I remember when, during the late war with China, a regiment left a certain town, a large concourse of people flocked to the station to bid farewell to the general and his army. On this occasion an American resident resorted to the place, expecting to witness loud demonstrations, as the nation itself was highly excited and there were fathers, mothers, wives, and sweethearts of the soldiers in the crowd. The American was strangely disappointed; for as the whistle blew and the train began to move, the hats of thousands of people were silently taken off and their heads bowed in reverential farewell; no waving of handkerchiefs, no word uttered, but deep silence in which only an attentive ear could catch a few broken sobs. In domestic life, too, I know of a father who spent whole nights listening to the breathing of a sick child, standing behind the door that he might not be caught in such an act of parental weakness! I know of a mother who, in her last moments, refrained from sending for her son, that he might not be disturbed in his studies. Our history and everyday life are replete with examples of heroic matrons who can well bear comparison with some of the most touching pages of Plutarch.

It is the same discipline of self-restraint which is accountable for the absence of more frequent revivals in the Christian churches of Japan. When a man or woman feels his or her soul stirred, the first instinct is to quietly suppress the manifestation of it. In rare instances is the tongue set free by an irresistible spirit, when we have eloquence of sincerity and fervor. It is putting a premium upon a breach of the third commandment to encourage speaking lightly of spiritual experience. It is truly jarring to Japanese ears to hear the most sacred words, the most secret heart experiences, thrown out in promiscuous audiences. "Dost thou feel the soil of thy soul stirred with tender thoughts? It is time for seeds to sprout. Disturb it not with speech; but let it work alone in quietness and secrecy," — writes a young samurai in his diary.

To give in so many articulate words one's inmost thoughts and feelings — notably the religious — is taken among us as an unmistakable sign that they are neither very profound nor very sincere. "Only a pomegranate is he" — so runs a popular saying — "who, when he gapes his mouth, displays the contents of his heart."

It is not altogether perverseness of oriental minds that the instant our emotions are moved we try to guard our lips in order to hide them. Speech is very often with us, as the Frenchman defined it, "the art of concealing thought."

Call upon a Japanese friend in time of deepest affliction and he will invariably receive you laughing, with red eyes or moist cheeks. At first you may think him hysterical. Press him for explanation and you will get a few broken commonplaces — "Human life has sorrow;" "They who meet must part;" "He that is born must die;" "It is foolish to count the years of a child that is gone, but a woman's heart will indulge in follies;" and the like.

The suppression of feelings being thus steadily insisted upon, they find their safety-valve in poetical aphorisms. A poet of the tenth century writes, "In Japan and China as well, humanity, when moved by sorrow, tells its bitter grief in verse." A mother who tries to console her broken heart by fancying her departed child absent on his wonted chase after the dragon-fly, hums,

"How far to-day in chase, I wonder,
Has gone my hunter of the dragon-fly!"

I hope I have in a measure shown that inner working of our minds which often presents an appearance of callousness or of an hysterical mixture of laughter and dejection, and whose sanity is sometimes called in question.

It has also been suggested that our endurance of pain and indifference to death are due to less sensitive nerves. This is plausible as far as it goes. The next question is, — Why are our nerves less tightly strung? It may be our climate is not so stimulating as the American. It may be our monarchical form of government does not excite us as much as the Republic does the Frenchman. I believe it was our very excitability and sensitiveness which made it a necessity to recognize and enforce constant self-repression; but whatever may be the explanation, without taking into account long years of discipline in self-control, none can be correct.

...the high estimate placed upon honor was ample excuse with many for taking one's own life.

The Institutions of Suicide and Redress

Hara-kiri has fascinated the world for over a century. It is self-sacrifice by disembowelment. Hara means midriff, in this context. Kiri means murder. Seppuku is self-murder. Often this ritualistic sacrifice is referred to as seppuku. The seat of the soul was believed to be in the intestines, hence the development of this unappetizing method of self-murder.

The high value placed on honor was the triggering mechanism that justified taking one's own life if honor was irretrievably destroyed.

> "When honor is lost, 'tis a relief to die,
> Death's but a sure retreat from infamy."

In Bushido death was a key to the solution of many complex problems.

Seppuku was a legal, ceremonial institution. It was a refinement of self-destruction. No one could perform it without the utmost coolness of temper and composed demeanor. It particularly befitted the profession of bushi.

For a true samurai to hasten death, or to court it, was cowardice. There was an exact parallel in Sir Thomas Brown's Religio Medici, "It is a brave act of valor to condemn death, but where life is more terrible than death it is then the truest valor to dare to live." The indoctrination of such an attitude curbed the popular over-use of seppuku in fledgling samurai.

When there were no criminal courts, murder was not a crime, and only the vigilant vengeance of the victim's people preserved social order. The threat of revenge was a barrier to anarchy and chaos. By means of revenge one's sense of justice was satisfied. The effort to achieve an exact balance and equal justice was like the Old Testament admonition, "An eye for an eye, a tooth for a tooth." Judaism had a vengeful God; Greek thought, a Nemesis. In other cultures vengeance was often left to some super-human agency. In Bushido the institution of redress served as a kind of ethical court of equity, where people took cases not able to be judged in accordance with ordinary law. The only Supreme Court in existence was vengeance.

Lao-tse taught to repay injury with kindness. But Confucius was much more influential: Injury must be recompensed with justice. Revenge was only justified when undertaken in behalf of superiors and benefactors. One's own wrongs were to be borne and forgiven.

When a criminal code was established for Japan both the institutions of suicide and of redress lost their purpose. The knight errantry of Miyamoto Musashi, often celebrated in chanbarra

films, became a romantic tale only of the past. (The role of
Musashi has been enacted by almost every Japanese actor. It is as
popular as the role of Hamlet is to English actors.)

Suicide is more of a romantic fantasy now than it is a practice
in Japan. Contemporary Japanese use the same means as anyone
else. Their rate is lower than many western countries. It must be
borne in mind that the samurai committed hara-kiri only as a
rational act, after careful consideration of all possible alternatives.
"If suicide is accomplished by very painful means or at the cost of
prolonged agony, in 99 of 100 cases, it may be termed the act of a
disordered mind, a mind disoriented by fanaticism or a mind
destroyed by morbid excitement," says Professor Morsell in his
studies of the Japanese culture.

THE INSTITUTIONS OF SUICIDE
AND REDRESS

The institutions of suicide *(hara-kiri)* and redress *(kataki-uchi)* have intrigued and mystified foreign writers for decades. Nevertheless, they have treated the subjects more or less fully.

To begin with suicide, let me state that I confine my observations only to *seppuku* or *kappuku*, popularly known as *hara-kiri* — which means self-immolation by disembowelment. "Ripping the abdomen? How absurd!" -- so cry those to whom the name is new. Absurdly odd as it may sound at first to foreign ears, it cannot be so very foreign to students of Shakespeare, who puts these words in Brutus' mouth — "Thy (Caesar's) spirit walks abroad and turns our swords into our proper entrails." In our minds it is associated with instances of noblest deeds and of most touching pathos, so that nothing repugnant, much less ludicrous, mars our conception of it. So wonderful is the transforming power of virtue, of greatness, of tenderness, that the vilest form of death assumes a sublimity and becomes a symbol of new life, or else — the sign which Constantine beheld would not conquer the world!

Not for extraneous associations only does *seppuku* lose in our mind any taint of absurdity; for the choice of this particular part of the body to operate upon, was based on an old anatomical belief as to the seat of the soul and of the affections. When Moses wrote of Joseph's "bowels yearning upon his brother," or David prayed the Lord not to forget his bowels, or when Isaish, Jeremiah, and other inspired men of old spoke of the "sounding" or the "troubling" of bowels, they all and each endorsed the belief prevalent among the Japanese that in the abdomen was enshrined the soul. The term *"hara"* was more comprehensive than the Greek *phren* or *thumos,* and the Japanese and Hellenese alike thought the spirit of man to dwell somewhere in that region. Such a notion is by no means confined to the peoples of antiquity. The French, in spite of the theory propounded by one of their most distinguished philosophers, Descartes, that the soul is located in the pineal gland, still insist in using the term *ventre* in a sense, which if anatomically too vague, is nevertheless physiologically significant. Similarly *entrailles* stands in their language for affection and compassion. Nor is such belief mere superstition, being more scientific than the general idea of making the heart the centre of the feelings. Modern neurologists speak of the abdominal and pelvic brains, denoting thereby sympathetic nerve centers in those parts which are strongly affected by any psychical action. This view of mental physiology once admitted, the syllogism of *seppuku* is easy to construct. "I will open the seat of my soul and show you how it fares with it. See for yourself whether it is polluted or clean."

I do not wish to be understood as asserting religious or even moral justification of suicide, but the high estimate placed upon honor was ample excuse with many for taking one's own life. How many acquiesced in the sentiment expressed by Garth,

"When honor's lost, 'tis a relief to die;
Death's but a sure retreat from infamy,"

and have smilingly surrendered their souls to oblivion! Death involving a question of honor, was accepted in Bushido as a key to the solution of many complex problems, so that to an ambitious samurai a natural departure from life seemed a rather tame affair and a consummation not devoutly to be wished for. I dare say that many good Christians, if only they are honest enough, will confess the fascination of, if not positive admiration for, the sublime composure with which Cato, Brutus, Petronius and a host of other ancient worthies, terminated their own earthly existence. Is it too bold to hint that the death of the first of the philosophers was partly suicidal? When we are told so minutely by his pupils how their master willingly submitted to the mandate of the state — which he knew was morally mistaken — in spite of the possibilities of escape, and how he took up the cup of hemlock in his own hand, even offering libation from its deadly contents, do we not discern in his whole proceeding and demeanor, an act of self-immolation? No physical compulsion here, as in ordinary cases of execution. True the verdict of the judges was compulsory: it said, "Thou shalt die, — and that by thy own hand." If suicide meant no more than dying by one's own hand, Socrates was a clear case of suicide. But nobody would charge him with the crime: Plato, who was averse to it, would not call his master a suicide.

Now my readers will understand that *seppuku* was not a mere suicidal process. It was an institution, legal and ceremonial. An invention of the middle ages, it was a process by which warriors could expiate their crimes, apologize for errors, escape from disgrace, redeem their friends, or prove their sincerity. When enforced as a legal punishment, it was practiced with due ceremony. It was a refinement of self-destruction, and none could perform it without the utmost coolness of temper and composure of demeanor, and for these reasons it was particularly befitting the profession of bushi.

Antiquarian curiosity, if nothing else, would tempt me to give here a description of this obsolete ceremonial; but seeing that such a description was made by a far abler writer, whose book is not much read now-a-days, I am tempted to make a somewhat lengthy quotation. Mitford, in his "Tales of Old Japan," after giving a translation of a treatise on *seppuku* from a rare Japanese manuscript, goes on to describe an instance of such an execution of which he was an eyewitness:—

"We (seven foreign representatives) were invited to follow the Japanese witness into the *hondo* or main hall of the temple, where the ceremony was to be performed. It was an imposing scene. A large hall with a high roof supported by dark pillars of wood. From the ceiling hung a profusion of those huge gilt lamps and ornaments peculiar to Buddhist temples. In front of the high altar, where the floor, covered with beautiful white mats, is raised some three or four inches from the ground, was laid a rug of scarlet felt. Tall candles placed at regular intervals gave out a dim mysterious light, just sufficient to let all the proceedings be seen. The seven Japanese took their places on the left of the raised floor, the seven foreigners on the right. No other person was present.

"After the interval of a few minutes of anxious suspense, Taki

Zenzaburo, a stalwart man thirty-two years of age, with a noble air, walked into the hall attired in his dress of ceremony, with the peculiar hempen-cloth wings which are worn on great occasions. He was accompanied by a *kaishaku* and three officers, who wore the *jimbaori* or war surcoat with gold tissue facings. The word *kaishaku*, it should be observed, is one to which our word executioner is no equivalent term. The office is that of a gentleman; in many cases it is performed by a kinsman or friend of the condemned, and the relation between them is rather that of principal and second than that of victim and executioner. In this instance, the *kaishaku* was a pupil of Taki Zenzaburo, and was selected by friends of the latter from among their own number for his skill in swordsmanship.

"With the *kaishaku* on his left hand, Taki Zenzaburo advanced slowly towards the Japanese witnesses, and the two bowed before them, then drawing near to the foreigners they saluted us in the same way, perhaps even with more deference; in each case the salutation was ceremoniously returned. Slowly and with great dignity the condemned man mounted on to the raised floor, prostrated himself before the high altar twice, and seated* himself on the felt carpet with his back to the high altar, the *kaishaku* crouching on his left-hand side. One of the three attendant officers then came forward, bearing a stand of the kind used in the temple for offerings, on which, wrapped in paper, lay the *wakizashi*, the short sword or dirk of the Japanese, nine inches and a half in length, with a point and an edge as sharp as a razor's. This he handed, prostrating himself, to the condemned man, who received it reverently, raising it to his head with both hands, and placed it in front of himself.

"After another profound obeisance, Taki Zenzaburo, in a voice which betrayed just so much emotion and hesitation as might be expected from a man who is making a painful confession, but with no sign of either in his face or manner, spoke as follows:—

"I, and I alone, unwarrantably gave the order to fire on the foreigners at Kobe, and again as they tried to escape. For this crime I disembowel myself, and I beg you who are present to do me the honor of witnessing the act.

"Bowing once more, the speaker allowed his upper garments to

*Seated himself — that is, in the Japanese fashion, his knees and toes touching the ground and his body resting on his heels. In this position, which is one of respect, he remained until his death.

slip down to his girdle, and remained naked to the waist. Carefully, according to custom, he tucked his sleeves under his knees to prevent himself from falling backward; for a noble Japanese gentleman should die falling forwards. Deliberately, with a steady hand he took the dirk that lay before him; he looked at it wistfully, almost affectionately; for a moment he seemed to collect his thoughts for the last time, and then stabbing himself deeply below the waist in the left-hand side, he drew the dirk slowly across to his right side, and turning it in the wound, gave a slight cut upwards. During this sickeningly painful operation he never moved a muscle of his face. When he drew out the dirk, he leaned forward and stretched out his neck; an expression of pain for the first time crossed his face, but he uttered no sound. At that moment, the *kaishaku*, who, still crouching by his side, had been keenly watching his every movement, sprang to his feet, poised his sword for a second in the air; there was a flash, a heavy, ugly thud, a crashing fall; with one blow the head had been severed from the body.

"A dead silence followed, broken only by the hideous noise of the blood throbbing out of the inert heap before us, which but a moment before had been a brave and chivalrous man. It was horrible.

"The *kaishaku* made a low bow, wiped his sword with a piece of paper which he had ready for the purpose, and retired from the raised floor; and the stained dirk was solemnly borne away, a bloody proof of the execution.

"The two representatives of the Mikado then left their places, and crossing over to where the foreign witnesses sat, called to us to witness that the sentence of death upon Taki Zenzaburo had been faithfully carried out. The ceremony being at an end, we left the temple."

The glorification of *seppuku* offered, naturally enough, no small temptation to its unwarranted committal. For causes entirely incompatible with reason, or for reasons entirely undeserving of death, hot-headed youths rushed into it as insects fly into fire; mixed and dubious motives drove more samurai to this deed than nuns into convent gates. Life was cheap — cheap as reckoned by the popular standard of honor. The saddest feature was that honor, which was always in the *agio*, so to speak, was not always solid gold, but alloyed with baser meals. No one circle in the Inferno will boast of greater density of Japanese population than the seventh, to which Dante consigns all victims of self-destruction!

And yet, for a true samurai to hasten death or to court it, was alike cowardice. A typical fighter, when he lost battle after battle and was pursued from plain to hill and from bush to cavern, found himself hungry and alone in the dark hollow of a tree, his sword blunt with use, his bow broken and arrows exhausted — did not the noblest of the Romans fall upon his own sword in Philippi under like circumstances? — deemed it cowardly to die, but with a fortitude approaching a Christian martyr's, cheered himself with an impromptu verse:

"Come! evermore come,
Ye dread sorrows and pains!
And heap on my burden'd back;
That I not one test may lack
Of what strength in me remains!"

This, then, was the Bushido teaching — Bear and face all calamities and adversities with patience and a pure conscience; for as Mencius* taught, "When Heaven is about to confer a great office on anyone, it first exercises his mind with suffering and his sinews and bones with toil; it exposes his body to hunger and subjects him to extreme poverty; and it confounds his undertakings. In all these ways it stimulates his mind, hardens his nature, and supplies his incompetencies." True honor lies in fulfilling Heaven's decree and no death incurred in so doing is ignominious, whereas, death to avoid what Heaven has in store is cowardly indeed! In that quaint book of Sir Thomas Browne's, *Religio Medici*, there is an exact English equivalent for what is repeatedly taught in our Precepts. Let me quote it: "It is a brave act of valor to condemn death, but where life is more terrible than death, it is then the truest valor to dare to live." This is but one of the numerous examples that tends to confirm the identity of the human species, notwithstanding an attempt so assiduously made to render the distinction between Christian and Pagan as great as possible.

We have thus seen that the Bushido institution of suicide was neither so irrational nor barbarous as its abuse strikes us at first sight. We will now see whether its sister institution of Redress — or call it Revenge, if you will — has its mitigating features. I hope I can dispose of this question in a few words, since a similar institution, or call it custom, if that suits you better, prevailed

*I use Dr. Legge's translation verbatim.

among all peoples and has not yet become entirely obsolete, as attested by the continuance of duelling and lynching. Why, did not an American captain challenge Esterhazy, that the wrongs of Dreyfus be avenged? Among a savage tribe which has no marriage, adultery is not a sin, and only the jealousy of a lover protects a woman from abuse: so in a time which has no criminal court, murder is not a crime, and only the vigilant vengeance of the victim's people preserves social order. "What is the most beautiful thing on earth?" said Osiris to Horus. The reply was, "To avenge a parent's wrongs," — to which a Japanese would have added, "and a master's."

In revenge there is something which satisfies one's sense of justice. The avenger reasons:— "My good father did not deserve death. He who killed him did great evil. My father, if he were alive, would not tolerate a deed like this: Heaven itself hates wrong-doing. It is the will of my father; it is the will of Heaven that the evil-doer cease from his work. He must perish by my hand: because he shed my father's blood, I, who am his flesh and blood, must shed the murderer's. The same Heaven shall not shelter him and me." The ratiocination is simple and childish, but it shows an innate sense of exact balance and equal justice. "An eye for an eye, a tooth for a tooth." Our sense of revenge is as exact as our mathematical faculty, and until both terms of the equation are satisfied we cannot get over the sense of something left undone.

In Judaism, which believed in a vengeful God, or in Greek thought, which provided a Nemesis, vengeance may be left to super-human agencies; but common sense furnished Bushido with the institution of redress as a kind of ethical court of equity, where people could take cases not to be judged in accordance with ordinary law. The master of the forty-seven Ronins was condemned to death: he had no court of higher instance to appeal to; his faithful retainers addressed themselves to Vengeance, the only Supreme Court existing; they in their turn were condemned by common law, — but the popular instinct passed a different judgment, and hence their memory is still kept as green and fragrant as are their graves at Sengakuji to this day.

Though Lao-tse taught to recompense injury with kindness, the voice of Confucius was very much louder, which taught that injury must be recompensed with justice; — and yet revenge was justified only when it was undertaken in behalf of our superiors and benefactors. One's own wrongs, including injuries done to wife and children, were to be borne and forgiven. A samurai could therefore fully sympathize with Hannibal's oath to avenge his country's wrongs, but he scorns James Hamilton for wearing in his girdle a handful of earth from his wife's grave, as an eternal incentive to avenge her wrongs on the Regent Murray.

Both of these institutions of suicide and redress lost their reason for existing with the development of the criminal code. No more do we hear of romantic adventures of a fair maiden as she tracks in disguise the murderer of her parent. No more can we witness tragedies of family vendetta enacted. The knight errantry of Miyamoto Musashi is now a tale of the past. The well-ordered police spies out the criminal for the injured party and the law metes out justice. The whole state and society will see that wrong is righted. The sense of justice satisfied, there is no need of *kataki-uchi*. If this had meant that "hunger of the heart which feeds upon the hope of glutting that hunger with the life blood of the victim," as a New England divine has described it, a few paragraphs in the Criminal Code would not so entirely have made an end of it.

As to *seppuku*, though it too has no existence *de jure*, we still hear of it from time to time, and shall continue to hear, I am afraid, as long as the past is remembered. Many painless and timesaving methods of self-immolation will come in vogue, as its followers are increasing with fearful rapidity throughout the world; but Professor Morselli will have to concede to *seppuku* an aristocratic position among them. He maintains that "when suicide is accomplished by very painful means or at the cost of prolonged agony, in ninety-nine cases out of a hundred, it may be assigned as the act of a mind disordered by fanaticism, by madness, or by morbid excitement."* But a normal *seppuku* does not savor of fanaticism, or madness or excitement, utmost *sang froid* being necessary to its successful accomplishment. Of the two kinds into which Dr. Strahan† divides suicide, the Rational or Quasi, and the Irrational or True, *seppuku* is the best example of the former type.

*Morseli, Suicide, p. 314.
†Suicide and Insanity.

The very possession of the dangerous instrument imparts to him a feeling and an air of self-respect and responsibility.

The Sword, the Soul of the Samurai

More than any other instrument the sword was the emblem of power and prowess. Mahomet proclaimed, "The sword is the key to Heaven and Hell." This statement echoed a widely current Japanese sentiment.

From the age of five, a boy chosen for the samurai class dressed in costume and carried a wooden sword. From then on, he was never without the weapon.

At 15, the boy was deemed a man. At that age he had independence of action. As a responsible person he took pride in the possession of suitable side arms.

To the young man, the sword symbolized loyalty and honor. The daito was the longer sword, the shoto, the shorter. Both were referred to as katana. The shorter was also occasionally called wakizashi.

The sword had a place of honor in the home. The samurai had it by his pillow at night. It was always within reach.

The sword was venerated, almost worshipped, like an icon. An insult to the sword was regarded as a personal affront. For example, one must never step over a weapon found lying on the floor.

Vanity of ownership of a samurai sword prompted the artist and craftsman who rendered the swords to attempt an inspirational masterpiece each time he made one of the valuable weapons. The swordsmith regarded his workshop as a sanctuary. He began each day with prayer and purification. "He committed his soul and spirit into forging and tempering the steel." Each believed that he infused the sword with the smith's tutelary god. Each sword had an immaculate texture, a flashing light bluish hue, a matchless edge and the curve of its back united exquisite grace and utmost strength.

Did Bushido justify the promiscuous use of the weapon? Never!! Unlike the heroes of the American West, the right time to use the weapon came only rarely for the samurai. One of the most respected samurai, the Count Katsu said, "I have a great dislike for killing people and so I haven't killed one single man . . . ." He believed in the adage he quoted so often, "The best won victory is that obtained without shedding blood."

THE SWORD, THE SOUL OF THE
SAMURAI

When Mahomet proclaimed that "The sword is the key of Heaven and of Hell," he only echoed a Japanese sentiment. Common people had ample reason to fear it, and the samurai boy early learned to wield it. It was a momentous occasion for him when at the age of five he was apparelled in the paraphernalia of samurai costume, placed upon a *go*-board* and initiated into the rights of the military profession, by having thrust into his girdle a real sword instead of the toy dirk he had been playing with. After this first ceremony of *adoptio per arma*, he was no more to be seen outside his father's gates without this badge of his status, even if it was usually substituted for everyday wear by a gilded wooden dirk. Not many years pass before he wears constantly the genuine steel, though blunt, and then the

*The game of *go* is sometimes called Japanese checkers, but is much more intricate than the English game. The *go*-board contains 361 squares and is supposed to represent a battle-field — the object of the game being to occupy as much space as possible.

sham arms are thrown aside and with enjoyment keener than his newly acquired blades, he marches out to try their edge on wood and stone. When he reaches man's estate at the age of fifteen, being given independence of action, he can now pride himself upon the possession of arms sharp enough for any work. The very possession of the dangerous instrument imparts to him a feeling and an air of self-respect and responsibility. "He beareth not his sword in vain." What he carries in his belt is a symbol of what he carries in his mind and heart, — Loyalty and Honor. The two swords, the longer and the shorter, — called respectively *daito* and *shoto* or *katana* and *wakizashi*, — never leave his side. When at home, they grace the most conspicuous place in study or parlor; by night they guard his pillow within easy reach of his hand. Constant companions, they are beloved, and proper names of endearment given them. Being venerated, they are well-nigh worshipped. The Father of History has recorded as a curious piece of information that the Scythians sacrificed to an iron scimitar. Many a temple and many a family in Japan hoards a sword as an object of adoration. Even the commonest dirk has due respect paid to it. Any insult to it is tantamount to personal affront. Woe to him who carelessly steps over a weapon lying on the floor!

So precious an object cannot long escape the notice and the skill of artists nor the vanity of its owner, especially in times of peace, when it is worn with no more use than a crosier by a bishop or a sceptre by a king. Sharkskin and finest silk for hilt, silver and gold for guard, lacquer of varied hues for scabbard, robbed the deadliest weapon of half its terror; but these appurtenances are playthings compared with the blade itself.

The swordsmith was not a mere artisan but an inspired artist and his workshop a sanctuary. Daily he commenced his craft with prayer and purification, or, as the phrase was, "he committed his soul and spirit into the forging and tempering of the steel." Every swing of the sledge, every plunge into water, every friction on the grindstone, was a religious act of no slight import. Was it the spirit of the master or of his tutelary god that cast a formidable spell over our sword? Perfect as a work of art, setting at defiance its Toledo and Damascus rivals, there was more than art could impart. Its cold blade, collecting on its surface the moment it is drawn the vapours of the atmosphere; its immaculate texture, flashing light of bluish hue; its matchless edge, upon which histories and possibilities hang; the curve of its back, uniting exquisite grace with utmost strength; — all these thrill us with mixed feelings of power and beauty, of awe and terror. Harmless were its mission, if it only remained a thing of beauty and joy! But, ever within reach of the hand, it presented no small temptation for abuse. Too often did the blade flash forth from its peaceful sheath. The abuse sometimes went so far as to try the acquired steel on some harmless creature's neck.

The question that concerns us most is, however, — Did Bushido justify the promiscuous use of the weapon? The answer is unequivocally, no! As it laid great stress on its proper use, so did it denounce and abhor its misuse. A dastard or a braggart was he who brandished his weapon on undeserved occasions. A self-possessed man knows the right time to use it, and such times come but rarely. Let us listen to the late Count Katsu, who passed through one of the most turbulent times of our history, when assassinations, suicides, and other sanguinary practices were the order of the day. Endowed as he once was with almost dictatorial powers, chosen repeatedly as an object of assassination, he never tarnished his sword with blood. In relating some of his reminiscences to a friend he says, in a quaint, plebeian way peculiar to him: — "I have a great dislike for killing people and so I haven't killed one single man. I have released those whose heads should have been chopped off. A friend said to me one day, 'You don't kill enough. Don't you eat pepper and egg-plants?' Well, some people are no better! But you see that fellow was slain himself. My escape may be due to my dislike of killing. I had the hilt of my sword so tightly fastened to the scabbard that it was hard to draw the blade. I made up my mind that though they cut me, I will not cut. Yes, yes! some people are truly like fleas and mosquitoes and they bite — but what does their biting amount to? It itches a little, that's all; it won't endanger life." These are the words of one whose Bushido training was tried in the fiery furnace of adversity and triumph. The popular apothegm — "To be beaten is to conquer," meaning true conquest consists in not opposing a riotous foe; and "The best won victory is that obtained without shedding of blood," and others of similar import — will show that after all the ultimate ideal of knighthood was Peace.

It was a great pity that this high ideal was left exclusively to priests and moralists to preach, while the samurai went on practicing and extolling martial traits. In this they went so far as to tinge the ideals of womanhood with Amazonian character.

Woman's surrender of herself to the good of the home and family was as willing and honorable as the man's self-surrender to the good of his lord and country.

The Training
and Position of Women

*The Chinese ideogram denoting "the mysterious," "the un-
knowable" is composed of two parts, one meaning "young," the
other, "woman." It was believed that the intuition of the female
of the species was beyond the comprehension of the male. The
Chinese ideogram representing a wife also depicted a woman
holding a broom.*

*In the Bushido ideal of woman, however, there was little
mystery and the image was similar to the one for the Precepts of
Knighthood where the ideal of domesticity was tinged with
Amazonian traits.*

*Bushido's code praised women "who emancipated themselves
from the frailty of their sex and displayed heroic fortitude worthy
of the strongest and bravest of men." The ideal parallels the
American Frontier or Pioneer woman more so than it does
contemporary women's lib.*

*Under Bushido, girls learned to repress their feelings, to harden
their nerves and to excel in weaponry. This was usually the
nagi-nata (long handled sword). The Bushido woman had no
overlord, so she learned to defend herself. Fencing kept her in
good health, gave her speed and endurance. The women following
the Bushido Code, carried kai-ken (long-bladed pocket daggers).
They carried these in their bosoms for defense, or if need be to
commit seppuka. It was a tradition that their greatest domestic
quality was in the education of their sons.*

*To smooth the angularity of movement the women learned
dancing. Music was essential as an art to regale weary hours of
husbands and fathers. Music, dance and poetry were only to purify
the heart. Under Bushido the woman surrendered herself to the
good of home and family in much the way the man accomplished
self-surrender to lord or country. Self-renunciation operated as a*

key-note of the loyalty of man and domesticity in woman. But there was never any sense of slavish surrender.

In the class structure of feudal Japanese society, women had more equality in lower classes where the husband and wife struggled along as co-equal partners in the fight for survival.

In the military class there were about 2,000,000 samurai. Above this military class were the military nobles and above them the court nobles. Below the samurai were the masses—mechanics, tradesmen, peasants—all of whom devoted their lives to the peaceful arts.

Among the higher ranking nobility the differences between the sexes were increasingly less marked. There were few occasions to bring the differences into prominence. The more leisurely nobles grew increasingly effeminate.

Under Bushido, woman was not regarded as man's equal. But men were not equal among themselves as demonstrated in courts of law, polling places and the like. On the battlefield a woman was expected to contribute little, at home everything.

For the woman in the Bushido ethic, life focused on the home as the center of the universe. The man focused his life on service to his lord and his Emperor.

To praise one's wife was thought to be in very bad taste. It was the equivalent of praising some part of yourself. Instead, there was polite debasement. In Western civilization, man paid respect for woman. It became a standard of morality. But under Bushido the water-shed between good and bad was along the line of duty binding man to his own divine soul and then to other souls in the relationships of master to servant, older to younger brother, friend to friend and Shintoism with Buddhism. These relationships were discussed in the first chapter of this book.

THE TRAINING AND POSITION OF
WOMAN

The female half of our species has sometimes been called the paragon of paradoxes, because the intuitive working of their mind is beyond the comprehension of men's "arithmetical understanding." The Chinese ideogram denoting "the mysterious," "the unknowable," consists of two parts, one meaning "young" and the other "woman," because the physical charms and delicate thoughts of the fair sex are above the coarse mental calibre of our sex to explain.

In the Bushido ideal of woman, however, there is little mystery and only a seeming paradox. I have said that it was Amazonian, but that is only half the truth. Ideographically the Chinese represent wife by a woman holding a broom — certainly not to brandish it offensively or defensively against her conjugal ally, neither for witchcraft, but for the more harmless uses for which the besom was first invented — the idea involved being thus not less homely than the etymological derivation of the English wife (weaver) and daughter (duhitar, milkmaid). Without confining the sphere of woman's activity to *Kuche, Kirche, Kinder*, as the recent German Kaiser was said to do, the Bushido ideal of womanhood was pre-eminently domestic. These seeming contradictions — Domesticity and Amazonian traits — are not inconsistent with the Precepts of Knighthood, as we shall see.

Bushido being a teaching primarily intended for the masculine sex, the virtues it prized in woman were naturally far from being distinctly feminine. Winckelmann remarks that "the supreme beauty of Greek art is rather male than female," and Lecky adds that it was true in the moral conception of the Greeks as in their art. Bushido similarly praised those women most "who emancipated themselves from the frailty of their sex and displayed an heroic fortitude worthy of the strongest and the bravest of men."[*] Young girls, therefore, were trained to repress their feelings, to indurate their nerves, to manipulate weapons, — especially the long-handled sword called *nagi-nata*, so as to be able to hold their own against unexpected odds. Yet the primary motive for exercise of this martial character was not for use in the field: it was two-fold — personal and domestic. Woman owning no suzerain of her own, formed her own body-guard. With her weapon she guarded her personal sanctity with as much zeal as her husband did his master's. The domestic utility of her warlike training was in the education of her sons, as we shall see later.

Fencing and similar exercises, if rarely of practical use, were a wholesome counterbalance to the otherwise sedentary habits of women. But these exercises were not followed only for hygienic purposes. They could be turned into use in times of need. Girls, when they reached womanhood, were presented with dirks

[*]Lecky, History of European Morals, II, p. 383.

(kai-ken, pocket poniards), which might be directed to the bosom of their assailants, or, if advisable, to their own. The latter was very often the case: and yet I will not judge them severely. Even the Christian conscience with its horror of self-immolation, will not be harsh with them, seeing Pelagia and Dominina, two suicides, were canonized for their purity and piety. When a Japanese Virginia saw her chastity menaced, she did not wait for her father's dagger. Her own weapon lay always in her bosom. It was a disgrace to her not to know the proper way in which she had to perpetrate self-destruction. For example, little as she was taught in anatomy, she must know the exact spot to cut in her throat: she must know how to tie her lower limbs together with a belt so that, whatever the agonies of death might be, her corpse be found in utmost modesty with the limbs properly composed. Is not a caution like this worthy of the Christian Perpetua or the Vestal Cornelia? I would not put such an abrupt interrogation, were it not for a misconception, based on our bathing customs and other trifles, that chastity is unknown among us.*

It would be unfair to give my readers an idea that masculinity alone was our highest ideal for woman. Far from it! Accomplishments and the gentler graces of life were required of them. Music, dancing and literature were not neglected. Some of the finest verses in our literature were expressions of feminine sentiments; in fact, women played an important role in the history of Japanese *belles lettres.* Dancing was taught (I am speaking of samurai girls and not of *geisha)* only to smooth the angularity of their movements. Music was to regale the weary hours of their fathers and husbands; hence it was not for the technique, the art as such, that music was learned; for the ultimate object was purification of heart, since it was said that no harmony of sound is attainable without the player's heart being in harmony with itself. Here again we see the same idea prevailing which we notice in the training of youths — that accomplishments were ever kept subservient to moral worth. Just enough of music and dancing to add grace and brightness to life, but never to foster vanity and extravagance. I sympathize with the Persian Prince, who, when taken into a ball-room in London and asked to take part in the merriment, bluntly remarked that in his country they provided a particular set of girls to do that kind of business for them.

*For a very sensible explanation of nudity and bathing see Finck's *Lotos Time in Japan,* pp. 286-297.

The accomplishments of our women were not acquired for show or social ascendancy. They were a home diversion; and if they shone in social parties, it was as the attributes of a hostess, — in other words, as a part of the household contrivance for hospitality. Domesticity guided their education. It may be said without fear of contradiction that the accomplishments of the women of Old Japan, be they martial or pacific in character, were mainly intended for the home; and, however far they might roam, they never lost sight of the hearth as the center. It was to maintain its honor and integrity that they slaved, drudged, and gave up their lives. Night and day, in tones at once firm and tender, brave and plaintive, they sang to their little nests. As daughter, woman sacrificed herself for her father, as wife for her husband, and as mother for her son. Thus from earliest youth she was taught to deny herself. Her life was a perpetual self-sacrifice. It is sometimes laid to the charge of our sex that we enslaved the womankind. I have once heard Socrates called the slave of conscience. If slavery means obedience or surrender of one's will, there is an honorable slavery in life.

Woman's surrender of herself to the good of the home and family, was as willing and honorable as the man's self-surrender to the good of his lord and country. Self-renunciation, without which no life-enigma can be solved, was the key-note of Loyalty of man as well as of Domesticity of woman. She was no more slave of man than was her husband of his liege-lord. My readers will not accuse me of undue prejudice in favor of slavish surrender of volition. I accept in a large measure the view advanced and defended with breadth of learning and profundity of thought by Hegel, that history is the unfolding and realization of freedom. The point I wish to make is that the whole teaching of Bushido was so thoroughly imbued with the spirit of self-sacrifice, that it was required not only of woman but of man. Hence, until the influence of its Precepts is entirely done away with, our society will not realize the view rashly expressed by an American exponent of woman's rights, who exclaimed, "May all the daughters of Japan rise in revolt against ancient customs!" Can such a revolt succeed? Will it improve the female status? Will the rights they gain by such a summary process repay the loss of that sweetness of disposition, that gentleness of manner, which are their present heritage? Was not the loss of domesticity on the part of Roman matrons followed by moral corruption too gross to mention? Can the American reformer assure us that a revolt of our daughters is the true course for their historical development to take? These are grave questions. Changes must and will come without revolts! In the meantime let us see whether the status of the fair sex under Bushido regimen was really so bad as to justify a revolt.

We hear much of the outward respect European knights paid to "God and the ladies," — the incongruity of the two terms making Gibbon blush; we are also told by Hallam that the morality of Chivalry was coarse, that gallantry implied illicit love. The effect of Chivalry on the weaker vessel was food for reflection on the part of philosophers, M. Guizot contending that Feudalism and Chivalry wrought wholesome influences, while Mr. Spencer tells us with a great deal of authority that in a militant society (and what is feudal society if not militant!) the position of woman is necessarily low, improving only as society becomes more industrial. Now is M. Guizot's theory true of Japan, or is Mr. Spencer's? In reply I might aver that both are right. The military class in Japan was restricted to the samurai, comprising nearly 2,000,000 souls. Above them were the military nobles — the *daimio*, and the court nobles — or *kugé;* these higher, sybaritical nobles being fighters only in name. Below them were masses of the common people — mechanics, tradesmen, and peasants — whose life was devoted to arts of peace. Thus what Herbert Spencer gives as the characteristics of a militant type of society may be said to have been exclusively confined to the samurai class, while those of the industrial type were applicable to the classes above and below it. This is well illustrated by the position of woman; for in no class did she experience less freedom than among the samurai. Strange to say, the lower the social class — as, for instance, among small artisans — the more equal was the position of husband and wife. Among the higher nobility, too, the difference in the relations of the sexes was less marked, chiefly because there were few occasions to bring the differences of sex into prominence, the leisurely nobleman having become literally effeminate. Thus Spencer's dictum was fully exemplified in Old Japan. As to Guizot's, those who read his presentation of a feudal community will remember that he had the higher nobility especially under consideration, so that his generalization applies to the *daimio* and the *kugé*.

I shall be guilty of gross injustice to historical truth if my words give one a very low opinion of the status of woman under Bushido. I do not hesitate to state that she was not treated as man's equal; but, until we learn to discriminate between differences and inequalities, there will always be misunderstandings upon this subject.

When we think in how few respects men are equal among themselves, *e.g.*, before law courts or voting polls, it seems idle to trouble ourselves with a discussion on the equality of sexes. When the American Declaration of Independence said that all men were created equal, it had no reference to their mental or physical gifts: it simply repeated what Ulpian long ago announced, that before the law all men are equal. Legal rights were in this case the measure of their equality. Were the law the only scale to measure the position of woman in a community, it would be as easy to tell where she stands as to give her avoirdupois in pounds and ounces. But the question is: Is there a correct standard in comparing the relative social position of the sexes? Is it right, is it enough to compare woman's status to man's, as the value of silver is compared with that of gold, and give the ratio numerically? Such a method of calculation excludes from consideration the most important kind of value which a human being possesses, namely, the intrinsic. In view of the manifold variety of requisites for making each sex fulfill its earthly mission, the standard to be adopted in measuring its relative position must be of a composite character; or to borrow from economic language, it must be a multiple standard. Bushido had a standard of its own and it was binomial. It tried to gauge the value of woman on the battle-field and by the hearth. There she counted for very little; here for all. The treatment accorded her corresponded to this double measurement:—as a social-political unit not much, while as wife and mother she received highest respect and deepest affection. Why among so military a nation as the Romans, were their matrons so highly venerated? Was it not because they were *matrona*, mothers? Not as fighters or lawgivers, but as their mothers did men bow before them. So with us. While fathers and husbands were absent in field or camp, the government of the household was left entirely in the hands of mothers and wives. The education of the young, even their defense, was entrusted to them. The warlike exercises of women, of which I have spoken, were primarily to enable them to intelligently direct and follow the education of their children.

I have noticed a rather superficial notion prevailing among half-informed foreigners, that because the common Japanese expression for one's wife is "my rustic wife" and the like, she is despised and held in little esteem. When it is told that such phrases as "my foolish father," "my swinish son," "my awkward self," etc., are in current use, is not the answer clear enough?

To me it seems that our idea of marital union goes in some ways further than the so-called Christian. "Man and woman shall be one flesh." The individualism of the Anglo-Saxon cannot let go of the idea that husband and wife are two persons; — hence when they disagree, their separate *rights* are recognized, and when they agree, they exhaust their vocabulary in all sorts of silly petnames and nonsensical blandishments. It sounds highly irrational to our ears, when a husband or wife speaks to a third party of his or her other half — better or worse — as being lovely, bright, kind, and what not. Is it good taste to speak of one's self as "my bright self," "my lovely disposition," and so forth? We think praising one's own wife is praising a part of one's own self, and self-praise is regarded, to say the least, as bad taste among us, — and I hope, among Christian nations too! I have diverged at some length because the polite debasement of one's consort was a usage most in vogue among the samurai.

The Teutonic races beginning their tribal life with a super-stitious awe of the fair sex (though this is really wearing off in Germany!), and the Americans beginning their social life under the painful consciousness of the numerical insufficiency of women* (who, now increasing, are, I am afraid, fast losing the prestige their colonial mothers enjoyed), the respect man pays to woman has in Western civilization become the chief standard of morality. But in the martial ethics of Bushido, the main water-shed dividing the good and the bad was sought elsewhere. It was located along the line of duty which bound man to his own divine soul and then to other souls in the five relations I have mentioned in the early part of this paper. Of these we have brought to our reader's notice, Loyalty, the relation between one man as vassal and another as lord. Upon the rest, I have only dwelt incidentally as occasion presented itself; because they were not peculiar to Bushido. Being founded on natural affections, they could but be common to all mankind. It is not surprising, however, that the virtues and

*I refer to those days when girls were imported from England and given in marriage for so many pounds of tobacco, etc.

teachings unique in the Precepts of Knighthood did not remain circumscribed to the military class.

"As among flowers the cherry is queen, so among men the samurai is lord."

Influence of Bushido

The ethical system of Bushido that enlightened and guided the military class attracted followers from everywhere. Its effects percolated through all of Japanese society.

Democracy raises a natural prince for its leader. Aristocracy infuses princely spirit among the people. In the Anglo-Saxon world, liberty did not develop from the masses, but from gentlemen. What Japan was she owed to the samurai. In English literature, stories and poems of the exploits of knights and nobles abound. Actually they were a very small class numerically. In Japan the tales of the samurai achieved the same literary stature.

Exploits of the samurai still dominate literature, poetry, songs, novels, motion picture fare and TV. It may be best summed up in a popular child's verse, "As among flowers the cherry is queen, so among men the samurai is lord."

Intellectual and moral Japan was either directly or indirectly the work of the samurai. Bushido was a way of life.

THE INFLUENCE OF BUSHIDO

We have brought into view only a few of the more prominent peaks which rise above the range of knightly virtues, in themselves so much more elevated than the general level of our national life. As the sun in its rising first tips the highest peaks with russet hue, and then gradually casts its rays on the valley below, so the ethical system which first enlightened the military order drew in course of time followers from amongst the masses. Democracy raises up a natural prince for its leader, and aristocracy infuses a princely spirit among the people. Virtues are no less contagious than vices. No social class or caste can resist the diffusive power of moral influence.

Prate as we may of the triumphant march of Anglo-Saxon liberty, rarely has it received impetus from the masses. Was it not rather the work of the squires and *gentlemen?* Very truly does M. Taine say, "These three syllables, as used across the channel, summarize the history of English society." Democracy may make self-confident retorts to such a statement and fling back the question — "When Adam delved and Eve span, where then was the gentleman?" All the more pity that a gentleman was not present in Eden!

What Japan was she owed to the samurai. They were not only the flower of the nation but its root as well. All the gracious gifts of Heaven flowed through them.

In the most chivalrous days of Europe, Knights formed numerically but a small fraction of the population, but, as Emerson says, — "In English Literature half the drama and all the novels, from Sir Philip Sidney to Sir Walter Scott, paint this figure (gentleman)." Write in place of Sidney and Scott, Chikamatsu and Bakin, and you have in a nutshell the main features of the literary history of Japan.

The innumerable avenues of popular amusement and instruction — the theatres, the storytellers' booths, the preacher's dais, the musical recitations, the novels, — have taken for their chief theme the stories of the samurai. The peasants round the open fire in their huts never tire of repeating the achievements of Yoshitsune and his faithful retainer Benkei, or of the two brave Soga brothers; the dusky urchins listen with gaping mouths until the last stick burns out and the fire dies in its embers, still leaving their hearts aglow with the tale that is told. The clerks and the shop boys, after their day's work is over and the *amado* (outside shutters) of the store are closed, gather together to relate the story of Nobunaga and Hidéyoshi far into the night, until slumber overtakes their weary eyes and transports them from the drudgery of the counter to the exploits of the field. The babe just beginning to toddle is taught to lisp the adventures of Momotaro, the daring conqueror of Ogreland. Even girls are so imbued with the love of knightly deeds and virtues that, like Desdemona, they would seriously incline to devour with greedy ear the romance of the samurai.

Samurai grew to be the *beau ideal* of the whole race. "As among flowers the cherry is queen, so among men the samurai is lord," so sang the populace. Debarred from commercial pursuits, the military class itself did not aid commerce; but there was no channel of human activity, no avenue of thought, which did not receive in some measure an impetus from Bushido. Intellectual and moral Japan was directly or indirectly the work of Knighthood.

Mr. Mallock, in his exceedingly suggestive book, "Aristocracy and Evolution," has eloquently told us that "social evolution, in so far as it is other than biological, may be defined as the unintended result of the intentions of great men;" further that historical progress is produced by a struggle "not among the community generally, to live, but a struggle amongst small sections of the community to lead, to direct, to employ, the majority in the best way." Whatever may be said about the soundness of his argument, these statements are amply verified in the part played by bushi in the social progress, as far as it went, of our Empire.

How the spirit of Bushido permeated all social classes is also shown in the development of a certain order of men, known as *otoko-daté*, the natural leaders of democracy. Staunch fellows were they, every inch of them strong with the strength of massive manhood. At once the spokesmen and the guardians of popular rights, they had each a following of hundreds and thousands of souls who proffered in the same fashion that samurai did to *daimio*, the willing service of "limb and life, of body, chattels and earthly honor." Backed by a vast multitude of rash and impetuous working men, these born "bosses" formed a formidable check to the rampancy of the two-sworded order.

In manifold ways has Bushido filtered down from the social class where it originated, and acted as leaven among the masses, furnishing a moral standard for the whole people. The Precepts of

Knighthood, begun at first as the glory of the élite, became in time an aspiration and inspiration to the nation at large; and though the populace could not attain the moral height of those loftier souls, yet *Yamato Damashi* (the soul of Japan) ultimately came to express the *Volksgeist* of the Empire. If religion is no more than "Morality touched by emotion," as Matthew Arnold defines it, few ethical systems are better entitled to the rank of religion than Bushido. Motoöri has put the mute utterance of the nation into words when he sings: —

> Isles of blest Japan!
> Should your Yamato spirit
> Strangers seek to scan,
> Say — scenting morn's sunlit air,
> Blows the cherry wild and fair!

Yes, the *sakura** has for ages been the favorite of our people and the emblem of our character. Mark particularly the terms of definition which the poet uses, the words the *wild cherry flower scenting the morning sun.*

The Yamato spirit is not a tame, tender plant, but a wild — in the sense of natural — growth; it is indigenous to the soil: its accidental qualities it may share with the flowers of other lands, but in its essence it remains the original, spontaneous outgrowth of our clime. But its nativity is not its sole claim to our affection. The refinement and grace of its beauty appeal to *our* aesthetic sense as no other flower can. We cannot share the admiration of the Europeans for their roses, which lack the simplicity of our flower. Then, too, the thorns that are hidden beneath the sweetness of the rose, the tenacity with which she clings to life, as though loath or afraid to die rather than drop untimely, preferring to rot on her stem; her showy colors and heavy odors — all these are traits so unlike our flower, which carries no dagger or poison under its beauty, which is ever ready to depart life at the call of nature, whose colors are never gorgeous, and whose light fragrance never palls. Beauty of color and of form is limited in its showing: it is a fixed quality of existence, whereas fragrance is volatile, ethereal as the breathing of life. So in all religious ceremonies frankincense and myrrh play a prominent part. There is something spiritual in emitting aromas. When the delicious perfume of the cherry tree *(sakura)* quickens the morning air, as the sun in its course rises to illumine first the isles of the Far East, few sensations are more serenely exhilarating to inhale.

**Cerasus pseudo-cerasus*, Lindley.

When the Creator himself is pictured as making new resolutions in his heart upon smelling a sweet savor (Gen. VIII, 21), is it any wonder that the sweet-smelling season of the cherry blossom should call forth the whole nation from their little habitations? Blame them not if for a time their limbs forget their toil and their hearts their pangs and sorrows. Their brief pleasure ended, they return to their daily tasks with new strength and new resolutions. Thus in ways more than one is the sakura the flower of the nation.

"... the firm rock which the waters must wash day by day for centuries, before they can wear away even its external roughness."

Is Bushido Still Alive?

Most students of anthropology concede that the Code of Bushido survives even in the modern Westernized Japan. So imbedded was Bushido in the national character that it survived the wars of conquest and defeat of the Twentieth Century. But it has emerged in a greatly modified state from what has been described here. It has been described as like the indomitable rocks that withstand the rush of water. They are inevitably changed.

However unformulated it may be, Bushido was and still is the single animating spirit that is the motor force of Japan.

Today one can see in the student the same passion for loyalty and patriotism to causes that infused the way of the samurai. The student is regarded as the guardian of national honor.

By arousing the sentiments nurtured by Bushido, an effective moral renovation can be accomplished in any area of Japanese life.

IS BUSHIDO STILL ALIVE?

Or has Western civilization, in its march through the land, already wiped out every trace of this ancient discipline — Bushido?

It were a sad thing if a nation's soul could die so fast. That were a poor soul that could succumb so easily to foreign influences. The aggregate of psychological elements which constitute a national character is as tenacious as the "irreducible elements of species, of the fins of fish, of the beak of the bird, of the tooth of the carnivorous animal." In his recent book, full of shallow assertions and brilliant generalizations, M. LeBon* says, "The discoveries due to the intelligence are the common heritage of humanity; qualities

*The Psychology of Peoples, p. 33.

or defects of character constitute the exclusive heritage of each people: they are the firm rock which the waters must wash day by day for centuries, before they can wear away even its external roughness." These are strong words and would be highly worth pondering over, provided there were qualities and defects of character which *constitute the exclusive heritage* of each people. Schematizing theories of this sort had been advanced long before LeBon began to write his book, and they were exploded long ago by Theodor Waitz and Hugh Murray. In studying the various virtues instilled by Bushido, we have drawn upon European sources for comparison and illustrations, and we have seen that no one quality of character was its *exclusive heritage*. It is true the aggregate of moral qualities presents a quite unique aspect. It is this aggregate which Emerson names a "compound result into which every great force enters as an ingredient." But, instead of making it, as LeBon does, an exclusive heritage of a race or people, the Concord philosopher calls it "an element which unites the most forcible persons of every country; makes them intelligible and agreeable to each other; and is somewhat so precise that it is at once felt if an individual lack the Masonic sign."

The character which Bushido stamped on our nation and on the samurai in particular, cannot be said to form "an irreducible element of species," but nevertheless as to the vitality which it retains there is no doubt. Were Bushido a mere physical force, the momentum it has gained in the last seven hundred years could not stop so abruptly. Were it transmitted only by heredity, its influence must be immensely widespread. Just think, as M. Cheysson, a French economist, has calculated, that supposing there be three generations in a century, "each of us would have in his veins the blood of at least twenty million of the people living in the year 1000 A.D." The merest peasant that grubs the soil, "bowed by the weight of centuries," has in his veins the blood of ages, and is thus a brother to us as much as "to the ox."

An unconscious and irresistible power, Bushido has been moving the nation and individuals. It was an honest confession of the race when Yoshida Shôin, one of the most brilliant pioneers of Modern Japan, wrote on the eve of his execution the following stanza:

> Full well I knew this course must end in death:
> It was Yamato spirit urged me on
> To dare whate'er betide.

Unformulated, Bushido was and still is the animating spirit, the motor force of our country.

Mr. Ransome says that "there are three distinct Japans in existence side by side today, — the old, which has not wholly died out; the new, hardly yet born except in spirit; and the transition, passing now through its most critical throes." While this is very true in most respects, and particularly as regards tangible and concrete institutions, the statement, as applied to fundamental ethical notions, requires some modification; for Bushido, the maker and product of Old Japan, is still the guiding principle of the transition and will prove the formative force of the new era.

The great statesmen who steered the ship of our state through the hurricane of the Restoration and the whirlpool of national rejuvenation, were men who knew no other moral teaching than the Precepts of Knighthood. Some writers* have tried to prove that the Christian missionaries contributed an appreciable quota to the making of New Japan. I would fain render honor to whom honor is due: but this honor can hardly be accorded to the good missionaries. More fitting it will be to their profession to stick to the scriptural injunction of preferring one another in honor, than to advance a claim in which they have no proofs to back them. Whatever they do is still of an indirect effect. No, as yet Christian missions have effected but little visible in moulding the character of New Japan. No, it was Bushido, pure and simple, that urged us on for prosperity and health or disaster. Open the biographies of the makers of Modern Japan — of Sakuma, of Saigo, of Okubo, of Kido, not to mention the reminiscences of Ito, Okuma and Itagaki and you will find that it was under the impetus of samuraihood that they thought and wrought.

The transformation of Japan is a fact patent to the whole world. In a work of such magnitude various motives naturally entered; but if one were to name the principal, one would not hesitate to name Bushido. When we opened the whole country to foreign trade, when we introduced the latest improvements in every department of life, when we began to study Western politics and sciences, our guiding motive was not the development of our physical resources and the increase of wealth; much less was it a blind imitation of Western customs. The sense of honor which cannot bear being looked down upon as an inferior power,—that

*Speer: Missions and Politics in Asia, Lecture IV, pp. 189-192.
*Dannis: Christian Missions and Social Progress, Vol. I, p. 32, Vol. II, 70, etc.

was the strongest of motives. Pecuniary or industrial consider-
ations were awakened later in the process of transformation.

The influence of Bushido is still so palpable that he who doubts
may read. A glimpse into Japanese life will make it manifest. Read
Hearn, the most eloquent and truthful interpreter of the Japanese
mind, and you see the working of that mind to be an example of
the working of Bushido. The universal politeness of the people,
which is the legacy of knightly ways, is too well-known to be
repeated. The physical endurance, fortitude and bravery that "the
little Jap" possesses were sufficiently proved in the Chino-
Japanese war.* "Is there any nation more loyal and patriotic?" is a
question asked by many; and for the proud answer, "There is
not," we must thank the Precepts of Knighthood.

On the other hand, is it fair to recognize that for the faults and
defects of our character, Bushido is largely responsible. Our lack
of abstruse philosophy — while some of our young men have
already gained international reputation in scientific researches, not
one has achieved anything in philosophical lines — is traceable to
the neglect of metaphysical training under Bushido's regimen of
education. Our sense of honor is responsible for our exaggerated
sensitiveness and touchiness; and if there is the conceit in us with
which some foreigners charge us, that, too, is a pathological
outcome of honor.

Have you seen in your tour of Japan many a young man with
unkempt hair, dressed in shabbiest garb, carrying in his hand a
large cane or a book, stalking about the streets with an air of utter
indifference to mundane things? He is the *shosei* (student), to
whom the earth is too small and the Heavens are not high enough.
He has his own theories of the universe and of life. He dwells in
castles of air and feeds on ethereal words of wisdom. In his eyes
beam the fire of ambition: his mind is athirst for knowledge.
Penury is only a stimulus to drive him onward; worldly goods are
in his sight shackles to his character. He is the repository of
Loyalty and Patriotism. He is the self-imposed guardian of
national honor. With all his virtues and his faults, he is the last
fragment of Bushido.

Deep-rooted and powerful as is still the effect of Bushido, I
have said that it is an unconscious and mute influence. The heart
of the people responds, without knowing a reason why, to any

*Among other works on the subject, read Eastlake and Yamada on "Heroic Japan,"
and Diosy on "The New Far East."

appeal made to what it has inherited, and hence the same moral idea expressed in a newly translated term and in an old Bushido term, has vastly different degrees of efficacy. A backsliding Christian, whom no pastoral persuasion could help from downward tendency, was reverted from his course by an appeal made to his loyalty, the fidelity he once swore to his Master. The word "Loyalty" revived all the noble sentiments that were permitted to grow lukewarm. A band of unruly youths engaged in a long continued "students' strike" in a college, on account of their dissatisfaction with a certain teacher, disbanded at two simple questions put by the Director. — "Is your professor a blameless character? If so, you ought to respect him and keep him in the school. Is he weak? If so, it is not manly to push a falling man." The scientific incapacity of the professor, which was the beginning of the trouble, dwindled into insignificance in comparison with the moral issues hinted at. By arousing the sentiments nurtured by Bushido, moral renovation of great magnitude can be accomplished.

One cause of the failure of mission work is that most of the missionaries are entirely ignorant of our history — "What do we care for heathen records?" some say — and consequently estrange their religion from the habits of thought we and our forefathers have been accustomed to for centuries past. Mocking a nation's history — as though the career of any people — even of the lowest African savages possessing no record — were not a page in the general history of mankind. To a philosophic and pious mind the races themselves are marks of Divine calligraphy clearly traced in black and white as on their skin; and if this simile holds good, the yellow race forms a precious page inscribed in hieroglyphics of gold! Ignoring the past career of a people, missionaries claim that Christianity is a new religion, whereas, to my mind, it is an "old, old story." Christianity in its American or English form — with more of Anglo-Saxon freaks and fancies than grace and purity of its founder — is a poor scion to graft on Bushido stock. Should the propagator of the new faith uproot the entire stock, root and branches, and plant the seeds of the Gospel on the ravaged soil?

Whatever may be the error committed by individuals, there is little doubt that the fundamental principle of the religion they profess is a power which we must take into account in reckoning.

Scratch a Japanese of the most advanced ideas, and he will show a Samurai.

The Future of Bushido

It is feared that Bushido, like the European Code of Chivalry, may not survive into the Twenty-first Century. In Europe, chivalry was weaned from feudalism and adopted by the church. It had a new lease on life. In Japan, no religion was large enough to encompass Bushido. When the mother institution of feudalism was gone, it had to shift for itself. Industrialization caused a decay in the ceremonial code. Bushido has become kind of an organization of a sacred trust for intellectual and cultural codes engulfing the remnant of what remains of the feudalistic Bushido Code.

In 1870 feudalism was abolished. In 1875 wearing the sword was prohibited. A vacuum was created. The yakuza clans grew up as a quasi-military set of secret societies to replace the cult of the samurai. Lesser systems of morals than those of Bushido, prevailed and carried the nation through the wars of conquest and the ignominy of defeat in the first half of the Twentieth Century.

Since that time the Code of Bushido has been resurrected. The great international prize winning novelist Yukio Mishima lived and died by his contemporary conception of the code of Bushido.

In 1975 Takakura Ken, Japan's number one box office star of yakuza films said, "It's too hard in today's modern world to live your life according to Bushido. Too difficult. It's like a model for my life, maybe. For example, after Mishima killed himself, I felt like there was a man true to his beliefs. Let's say, I admire Bushido."

It is clear that no one movement so much infused the Japanese spirit and the entire Japanese way of life as did the still vaguely formulated Code of Bushido. Nevertheless, in spite of the pressures of a highly industrialized economy and a society breaking down the ceremonial culture of the past, the Code of Bushido can be everywhere observed as a part of the Japanese mind, spirit, culture and soul.

THE FUTURE OF BUSHIDO

Few historical comparisons can be more judiciously made than between the Chivalry of Europe and the Bushido of Japan, and, if history repeats itself, it certainly will do with the fate of the latter what it did with that of the former. The particular and local causes for the decay of Chivalry which St. Palaye gives, have, of course, little application to Japanese conditions; but the larger and more general causes that helped to undermine Knighthood and Chivalry in and after the Middle Ages are as surely working for the decline of Bushido.

One remarkable difference between the experience of Europe and of Japan is, that whereas in Europe when Chivalry was weaned from Feudalism and was adopted by the Church, it obtained a fresh lease of life, in Japan no religion was large enough to nourish Bushido. When Feudalism was gone, Bushido had to shift for itself. An elaborate military organization might have taken it under its patronage, but we know that modern warfare can afford little room for its continuous growth. Shintoism, which fostered it in its infancy, is itself obsolete. The hoary sages of ancient China are being supplanted by the intellectual parvenu of more modern philosophers. Moral theories of a comfortable kind, flattering to the Super-Nationalistic tendencies of the time, and therefore thought well-adapted to the need of this day, have been invented and propounded.

Governmental powers are arrayed against the Precepts of Knighthood. Already, as Veblen says, "the decay of the ceremonial code — or, as it is otherwise called, the vulgarization of life — among the industrial classes proper, has become one of the chief enormities of latter-day civilization in the eyes of all persons of delicate sensibilities." The irresistible tide of triumphant democracy, which can tolerate no form or shape of trust — and Bushido was a trust organized by those who monopolized reserve capital of intellect and culture, fixing the grades and value of moral qualities — is alone powerful enough to engulf the remnant of Bushido. The present societary forces are antagonistic to petty class spirit, and Chivalry is a class spirit. Modern society, if it pretends to any unity, cannot admit "purely personal obligations devised in the interests of an exclusive class."* Add to this the progress of popular instruction, of industrial arts and habits, of wealth and city-life, — then we can easily see that neither the keenest cuts of samurai's sword nor the sharpest shafts shot from Bushido's boldest bows can succeed. The state built upon the rock of Honor and fortified by the same — shall we call it the *Ehrenstaat?* — is fast falling into the hands of quibbling lawyers and gibbering politicians armed with logic-chopping engines of war.

Alas for knightly virtues! alas for samurai pride! Morality ushered into the world with the sound of bugles and drums, is destined to fade away as "the captains and the kings depart."

If history can teach us anything, the state built on martial virtues — be it a city like Sparta or an Empire like Rome — can never make on earth a "continuing city." Universal and natural as is the fighting instinct in man, fruitful as it has proved to be of noble sentiments and manly virtues, it does not comprehend the whole man. Beneath the instinct to fight there lurks a diviner instinct to love. We have seen that Shintoism, Mencius and Wan Yang Ming, have all clearly taught it; but Bushido and all other militant types of ethics, engrossed doubtless, with questions of immediate practical need, too often forgot to duly emphasize this fact. Life has grown larger in these latter times. Callings nobler and

*Norman Conquest, Vol. V, p. 482.

broader than a warrior's claim our attention today. Though war clouds hang heavy upon our horizon, we will believe that the wings of the angel of peace can disperse them. A nation that sells its birthright of peace, and backslides from the front rank of Industrialism into the file of Filibusterism, makes a poor bargain indeed!

When the conditions of society are so changed that they have become not only adverse but hostile to Bushido, it is time for it to prepare for an honorable burial. It is just as difficult to point out when chivalry dies, as to determine the exact time of its inception. Dr. Miller says that Chivalry was formally abolished in the year 1559, when Henry II of France was slain in a tournament. With us, the edict formally abolishing Feudalism in 1870 was the signal to toll the knell of Bushido. The edict, issued five years later, prohibiting the wearing of swords, rang out the old, "the unbought grace of life, the cheap defence of nations, the nurse of manly sentiment and heroic enterprise," it rang in the new age of "sophisters, economists, and calculators."

It has been said that Japan won her late war with China by means of Murata guns and Krupp cannon; it has been said the victory was the work of a modern school system; but these are less than half truths. Does ever a piano, be it of the choicest workmanship of Erhard or Stanley, burst forth into the Rhapsodies of Liszt or the Sonatas of Beethoven without a master's hand? Or, if guns win battles, why did not Louis Napoleon beat the Prussians with his machine guns, or the Spaniards with their Mausers the Filipinos, whose arms were no better than the old-fashioned Remingtons? The most improved guns and cannon do not shoot of their own accord; the most modern educational system does not make a coward a hero. No! What won the battles on the Yalu, in Korea and Manchuria, was the ghosts of our fathers, guiding our hands and beating in our hearts. They are not dead, those ghosts, the spirits of our warlike ancestors. To those who have eyes to see, they are clearly visible. Scratch a Japanese of the most advanced ideas, and he will show a samurai. If you would plant a new seed in his heart, stir deep the sediment which has accumulated there for ages, — or else, new phraseology reaches no deeper than his arithmetical understanding.

It has been predicted — and predictions have been corroborated by the events of the last half century — that the moral system of Feudal Japan, like its castles and its armories, will crumble into dust, and new ethics rise phoenix-like to lead New Japan in her path of progress. Desirable and probable as the fulfillment of such a prophecy is, we must not forget that a phoenix rises only from its own ashes, and that it is not a bird of passage. The seeds of the Kingdom, as vouched for and absorbed by the Japanese mind, blossomed in Bushido. Now its days are closing — sad to say, before its full fruition — and we turn in every direction for other sources of strength and comfort, but among them there is as yet nothing found to take its place. The profit and loss philosophy of Utilitarians and Materialists finds favor among logic-choppers with half a soul. The only other ethical system which is powerful enough to cope with Utilitarianism and Materialism is Christianity; but as yet it has not divested itself of foreign accoutrements.

Christianity and Materialism (including Utilitarianism) — or will the future reduce them to still more archaic forms of Hebraism and Hellenism? — will divide the world between them. Lesser systems of morals will ally themselves to either side for their preservation. On which side will Bushido enlist? Having no set dogma or formula to defend, it can afford to disappear as an entity; like the cherry blossom, it is willing to die at the first gust of the morning breeze. But a total extinction will never be its lot. Who can say that stoicism is dead? It is dead as a system; but it is alive as a virtue: its energy and vitality are still felt through many channels of life — in the philosophy of Western nations, in the jurisprudence of all the civilized world.

Bushido as an independent code of ethics may vanish, but its power will not perish from the earth; its schools of martial prowess or civic honor may be demolished, but its fight and its glory will long survive their ruins. Like its symbolic flower, after it is blown to the four winds, it will still bless mankind with the perfume with which it will enrich life. Ages after, when its customaries will have been buried and its very name forgotten, its odors will come floating in the air as from a far-off unseen hill, "the wayside gaze beyond;" — then in the beautiful language of the Quaker poet,

"The traveler owns the grateful sense
Of sweetness near, he knows not whence,
And, pausing, takes with forehead bare
The benediction of the air."